MEXICO
bY MOTORCYCLE:
AN ADVENTURE STORY AND GUIDE

By William B. Kaliher

MEXICO
bY MOTORCYCLE:
AN ADVENTURE STORY AND GUIDE

By William B. Kaliher

Kaliher, William B., 1945-
Mexico by Motorcycle: An Adventure Story and Guide

Includes index, map and photographs
ISBN 978-0-9735191-7-4

ISBN 978-0-9735191-7-4
First Edition 2015
Text, map and photographs by William B. Kaliher, unless other-
wise indicated

Cover design by Ana María Calatayud

Sombrero Books, P.O. Box 4, Ladysmith, B.C., V9G 1A , Canada

Acknowledgements

I've enjoyed the adventure and experience of motorcycling Mexico. The Mexican people have my love and appreciation for the kindness, warmth, knowledge and smiles they've bestowed on me during many visits. I want to thank Graeme Lydford, an Australian musician, writer, adventurer and thinker; Steve Vassey, author; Susan Plunkett, RN, Public Health Nurse, and many members of the South Carolina Writer's Workshop. These people freely gave their time and energy to refine, harness and improve what writing talent I possess.

I also wish to thank Dr. J. D. Robinson, Ms. Barbara Purvis, author, and Mr. Richard Wright, editor, for encouraging me to write. Mr. Barry M. Bragg provided many of the photographs from Yucatán.

Last, I need to thank my wife and sons for allowing me the freedom to occasionally become a vagabond.

Contents

Section IV
1971 - Revisiting the Past

Section V
Finishing the Ride

Section VI
Appendices

List of Photographs

List of Photographs   xi

List of Photographs   xiii

Introduction

It's three in the morning and I don't speak the language. What's worse – my lack of fluency isn't the main problem. Drizzle cutting the fog does nothing to ease the anxiety-induced perspiration soaking the Mexican truckers and farmers crowded together on the narrow, serpentine road. Not a woman or child is to be seen. They're huddled helplessly in truck cabs. Giant rocks echo, each cracking like individual lightning strikes across the shrouded mountains. Every man strains to see upward. Clack –clack – then more clacks in the distant night signaling huge stones coalescing into a cascade of gigantic rocks rumbling down mountainsides. The pungency of my own fright-induced sweat might overwhelm their odors, but no one cares. We glance at the two thousand-foot drop-off, then up and down the road, before darting behind the nearest big rig once again.

The horrific sounds stop and a tangible stillness fills the night. We wait for our hearts to slow and our breathing to become normal. Then it's relieved grins all around. Laughter and slaps on the back from my new buddies precede a great deal of rapid explanation. I don't understand a single word, but the tenor carries the meaning. It'll be ten or fifteen minutes — twenty if we're lucky— before the next avalanche and we repeat our futile retreat. Each time, I laugh at myself for seeking safety behind a semi. There would be as much hope of damming the Mississippi with the rig as using it to stop those huge tumbling boulders.

* * * * *

The scene described above occurred on my first motorcycle ride through Mexico in June, 1971. The roads have greatly improved since then, reducing the chance of avalanche. Still, rock slides are only one potential hazard you may encounter, and few are as dramatic as tumbling boulders.

I've traveled Mexico by virtually all-possible methods since 1964. A tour by motorcycle can be exciting, rewarding and challenging. In 1971, I rode from Columbia, South Carolina, to Yucatán, Mexico, on a SL Honda 175. I spent more than two months touring the country. The total trip exceeded ten thousand miles.

In 1993, at age forty-eight, I again ventured south by motorcycle. From El Paso, Texas, I cycled as far south as Oaxaca. That trip, on a Honda Nighthawk 250, was over 4,000 miles. Both trips were solo. Those grand tours and other shorter bike rides taught me many aspects of motorcycling and visiting south of the border that should be useful to anyone.

Aside from the border crossing and deciding what sites you want to visit, there are five major considerations for a biker traveling in Mexico: the size and type motorcycle, clothing, roads, driving conditions and the people (this means you as much as them). Addressing these issues before leaving will reduce the chance of unpleasant problems. This guide will provide useful information on each of those topics.

I've purposely written this guidebook differently. You're going to ride with me on this adventure. While this is a motorcycle story, it will assist anyone planning to travel Mexico. In the first section of the

1. Many mountain roads are shoulderless and drop off steeply. This highway is located between Veracruz and Oaxaca.

book, I suggest what and what not to do. Each advice chapter is highlighted with an experience from my own travels. If you just want to enjoy the ride, skip to Section Two. But, the following pages are worthwhile before heading south.

The problems a "gringo" faces traveling by car are magnified for a person traveling solo on a motorcycle. I'll touch on issues ranging from cultural differences to the odd —to us— placement of traffic signs. My focus on potential problems should help the newcomer. However, I've found the occasional difficulties insignificant in comparison to the rewards.

Before we kick off, there are several rudimentary facts and observations to understand. Many of the basics concerning Mexico are not what most people assume. But, if you're patient, you'll find more favorable than unfavorable differences in the culture and people.

2. Map of Mexico
Motorcycle routes in 1971 and 1993

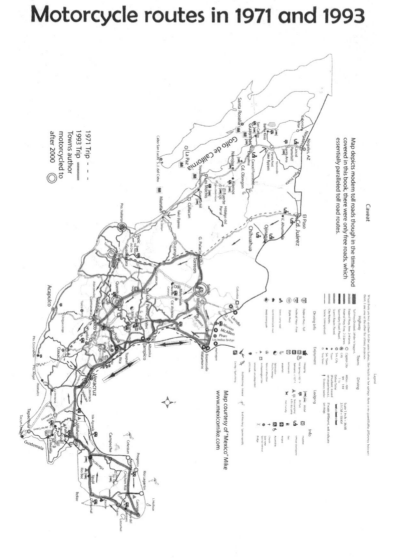

Map courtesy of "Mexico" Mike
www.mexicomike.com

Mexico by Motorcyle: An Adventure Story and Guide

Section I

Preparing for your Mexican Adventure

3. A lonely road slicing rural Yucatán.

1. The Basics of Preparation – Physical and Mental

The Right Motorcycle

A cracked and broken stone lane slanted steeply off to the left from where I rested at a roadside fruit stand. I was in high mountains and it was cold. I talked with some curious Indians sheathed in layers of brown, burlap-type ponchos. Several invited me, in broken Spanish, to visit their villages. I wondered what ancient pyramids and buried ruins lay down that rarely used path. The area was centrally located between several famous archaeological zones. The map showed two approximately parallel east-west roads north of the secondary road I was traveling. The closest was an incomplete dirt road perhaps fifty miles north with a paved road fifty miles beyond that. No other road or town marked that section of the map, not even the primitive lane urging me on.

I was on the edge of a huge, virtually unexplored area in modern Mexico. I badly wanted to answer the call to adventure. I knew less than a mile down the trail, ninety-nine percent of the people would have never seen a white man. Only a few would speak Spanish, much less English. If I went, I'd have to keep the hardiest two Indians with me. I would encounter at least two Indian languages, and perhaps others. There was no telling what never-before-seen

4. Section of the ruins at Ixtlán del Río.

ruins dotted the rugged area. With luck, I'd see rituals and lifestyles few people have witnessed. It would be an adventure rarely possible in the modern world.

Reality hit and utter disappointment broke my heart. I looked at my street bike and, for a second, even foolishly considered trying the road. I wanted to go, but there was no way. At most, I had two weeks left for exploration. If I were injured or used up my entire two weeks in this partially explored region, I needed a bike that could quickly bring me out. The street bike wouldn't have made it five miles on the rutted and cracked stone lane, even if I rode slowly. I explained I'd have to return another time. With great regret, I threw my leg over the bike, hit the starter button and eased onto the highway.

Deciding what bike you should take to Mexico is always difficult. On my trips, many people scoffed at the small size of my bikes for such long journeys. However, I safely and successfully made both trips, while many larger bikes never make a thousand miles in Mexico. The SL 175 allowed me to take many small, rough roads and trails I could only consider on the 250. With a 450 and up, I could never have contemplated many tantalizing side trips, even in the most perfect weather conditions. A combination trail and road bike is probably the best overall choice for someone traveling alone or who has never visited Mexico.

Ixtlán del Río is 149 km from Tepic.

*** La Sidra Spa** is 6 km from Ixtlán del Río.

It has two thermal water swimming pools and a restaurant.

The reality is that bike selection often depends on what you can afford, what you have at hand, how many people are going and how much time is available. Those factors will influence your decision. My comments on roads and traffic should be considered in conjunction with the following information when choosing your bike.

If you tour is strictly on paved roads and you're in a group, a larger bike is fine. If traveling solo or with one other person, a smaller bike should be considered. Long stretches of lonely roadway, easily a hundred miles, become a problem if you have mechanical trouble. A 250cc or smaller bike can be easily loaded onto a passing pickup and hauled to the next town. If you're sitting alone beside a cactus in the desert, you may not want to leave your $6,000-plus 750 while you seek help.

If you have trouble, even the smallest pueblos usually have a shade tree mechanic who will be of some aid. People still stop and help others along the roads. Twice a day, the government-sponsored Green Angels traverse major highways in a heavy truck with a variety of equipment to aid stranded motorists.

5. Curved wall, Ixtlán del Río ruins.

If you are going only a few hundred miles into Mexico to party at a beach resort, or if your time is limited, then I see no problem with a large street bike. Such a motorcycle is okay for all of Mexico if you recognize its inherent limitations. The country now has a series of expensive toll roads much like our interstates, which allows fairly easy street riding.

To put the motorcycle choice into perspective, consider the small archeological ruin, Ixtlán del Río, just off the excellent Highway 15, which runs from Guadalajara to the coast. One could not ask for a better mountain road for a large street bike. However, a few years ago, the ancient ruins would be almost inaccessible. Although they're only a few hundred yards off the highway, a huge railroad embankment cuts the access road. It's steep, and the tracks tall. There is little possibility of a street bike crossing without becoming lodged on the first rail.

If you are on a limited budget or are traveling to remote areas, all emphasis should be on your machine's size and ability. Its care becomes more important than clothes. If trouble arises, your bike is the one thing that can carry you home.

In conclusion, if you have a small or combination bike, use it. If not, use what you have, expecting some limitations to your exploration. The trip is so worthwhile! If I only had a scooter, the time and money for another trip, you might pass old Bill puttering along at 35 mph. But I'd be on the way to having the time of my life and another great adventure.

Basic Bike Requirements

If your planned trip will carry you beyond the main roads and cities, the following assortment of equipment is critical for roadside repairs.

1. Unless you are a good mechanic, don't travel to Mexico without a basic, easy-to-understand repair manual. If you don't have one, ask your dealer for the company's more detailed upkeep and minor repair manual.

   Also take:

2. A small flashlight that stores easily
3. An adjustable end wrench should supplement your bike's tool pouch
4. Extra fuses
5. A small can of oil
6. A couple of links to repair damaged chain
7. Extra spark plugs
8. A can of Fix-A-Flat (I've had a flat from a thorn)

Climate

Once, after visiting Mexico, I returned to work in late July. The summer back home had been one of the hottest in years. Temperatures had broken 100 degrees Fahrenheit for thirty days straight. A coworker welcomed me back exclaiming, "I'm so glad you're okay. I've been worried something happened to you with the heat down there."

He was serious and concerned, but had little understanding of Mexico. It only made sense it would be even warmer 1,500 miles to the south. I said, "Me? You should have worried I might freeze to death. I had to wear a jacket most nights, and two weeks ago, I wished I had a winter coat."

In Mexico, one must take into account both the seasons and elevation when anticipating the weather. Mexicans consider summer their worst season. Tropical storms hit the coasts during those months, making it the rainy season. The storm clouds expand over the mountain ranges and inland deluges can follow. My experience with the avalanche was the result of one of these tropical fronts. In 1971, there were no readily accessible Mexican weathercasts, but today such a situation can be easily avoided. By glancing at a forecast via cable television or a web site, the rider knows when to avoid secondary highways at high elevations.

The rain is only a slight drawback. For the most part, the weather is better than in many parts of the States. I don't recall precipitation ruining a single day in Mexico except when motorcycling high in the mountains. The rain can make the air uncomfortably cold. In most areas, precipitation is usually a brief sub-tropical downpour or just mist. It's not the type of rainfall that settles in for three or four days straight.

The real climate indicators have to do with elevation. Mexico is a mountainous country with most cities at high, cool elevations. Generally, going south, the first one or two hundred miles are desert and

6. Tall pine country on the famed Espinazo del Diablo route.

semi-desert. Once that band of barren landscape is crossed, the land and weather change greatly. There are snow covered mountains near Veracruz.

Mexico City is 7,400 feet above sea level. A traveler needs a sweater there and in many other cities during the evening. When riding, a motorcyclist often needs a jacket even during the day. In general, think in terms of perfect temperatures that can be chilly on a bike. However, the Mexico many of us imagine is found in the coastal and desert areas. Once a motorcyclist comes off the mountains onto the East Coast or the Yucatán, a tee shirt can feel like too much clothing. In these areas, the weather is like Savannah, Georgia or Charleston, South Carolina during late July. Hot and humid is normal, and seaside breezes offer the only escape from sweltering heat.

Clothing

The broken and tattered facades of buildings in Mexico can be misleading. You may think soiled stucco walls sheath the most abject poverty. Once you turn into a doorway, you may find families crowded together and chickens squawking on the ground floor. However, you may also turn into the most glorious courtyard imaginable. The vibrant flowers, singing birds, lush palms and other exotic plants can take your breath away. You'll envy the luxury and wish you could own such a colorfully tiled home in the States.

On my first motorcycle trip, I stopped in Torreón. Some college students from wealthy families decided to show me their town. We were walking beside a terrible looking building when the students invited me to attend a party that evening. I was wearing my last pair of jeans. They were filthy and crusted with road tar, and my tee shirt was overly ripe. My other clothes were hanging wet in my hotel room. They'd be dry when I returned, but far from stain-free. We turned and walked through a large, intricately carved doorway.

The ugly outside walls of the building held one of the most magnificent country clubs I'd ever entered. Gleaming wood shone everywhere. The interior four stories were uniquely constructed. No floor completely spanned the room. A grand piano stood on the stage at the second level. Broad staircases ran up to the other stories, each of which hosted its own chandelier. The stage could be viewed from any floor, including where we stood just inside the entrance. Despite the wonderfully different —to American eyes— design, and a multitude of unfamiliar adornments, I could only marvel at the architects and workmen who created such beauty. I ran my fingers over the rich, ornately handcrafted wood.

Of course, I wanted to attend the party, but my best clothes would make me look only a tad better

7. Interior garden —every home should have one.

than a street bum. I thought I'd stand out and be spurned. At the time, I didn't realize we North Americans, as Mexicans call us, are obvious no matter what we wear. However, the Mexican kids assured me my clothes would be no problem. They realized I was on an adventure and allowances could and would be made. With some trepidation, I later donned clean clothes and went to the party. Thankfully, the evening light didn't show the stains to maximum effect.

The orchestra was not something I was used to, but it and the party were great. People went out of their way to be sure I was enjoying myself and getting enough to eat and drink. They were full of questions about America and my trip. The Mexican men expressed the same desire many American men have but never do. It seems every man —if not most women— secretly longs to take an extended motorcycle trip.

Clothes always have to be a consideration for a biker, for unexpected situations can arise in Mexico.

I recommend as a minimum a warm leather jacket, a warm sweater (if there's space), a rain suit, two pairs of jeans (in addition to the pair you're wearing), four short-sleeve or tee shirts, six changes of socks and underclothes, a pair of shorts that can serve as a bathing suit, one pair of pants for fine dining (if you have room) and two-long sleeve shirts. One shirt should be reserved to go with the dress slacks. I stress the importance of one good shirt. You never know when a special opportunity will arise. I use the second long-sleeve shirt strictly to protect my arms from sunburn while riding.

Cleaning clothes is generally more expensive and more difficult than in the United States. There are four choices: hotels, laundromats and —in the most remote areas— village women pounding clothes on river rocks or washing them by hand. My favorite method is having clothes cleaned in a river. I am always amazed at how clean they get clothes by hand. I don't find a savings in the cost of cleaning, but it helps the villagers. The better hotels have cleaning services, but they are expensive.

I store my dirty clothes in a plastic bag until I have enough for a laundry visit. Most laundromats are located in working class neighborhoods or in difficult to reach downtown locations. You usually put your clothes in one day and retrieve them the next. Make sure the employees understand you want your clothes the next day and expect to get them late the following afternoon. If you plan to use laundromats or wash your own clothes, try to bring more tee shirts, socks and underwear than the minimum I recommended if you have space. Additionally, you can often find three for ten-dollar tee shirts in local markets. If you have the money, it can be worthwhile to just buy tee shirts as you go.

The need for a rain suit and a warm jacket may seem surprising, but parts of a bike trip can be utterly miserable without them. Most of Mexico is mountainous, and some peaks are snow covered year round. Mexico City is 7,400 feet and Zacatecas is 8,200 feet above sea level. A warm sweater is sufficient for Mexico City at night, but a coat might be needed in Zacatecas even during July. If your journey is strictly on the East Coast of Mexico and Yucatán, a light windbreaker is all you would need for the weather. On the Pacific coast, not much more is needed, but I would recommend a sweater.

Once you've packed your clothes and other necessary items, add any clothes you can throw away to the remaining space. As you ride through Mexico you'll see many rural and poverty-ridden pueblos just off the highways. Wear your throwaway clothes first. Once they're dirty, give them to the poor people. If you're shy about asking someone at a village if they can use some old clothes, just leave them on a mesquite bush near a pueblo. The clothes will find their way into the right hands and be appreciated. On my last bike ride, I took several old shirts simply to leave behind.

Safety

I've never felt unsafe in Mexico except early on, when I knew nothing about the people. I've been cheated once. I've had a cheap camera stolen in Mexico City when I foolishly set it down, and a computer stolen from my room in a smaller city, but over five decades I've never felt in physical danger. The best I can do is relate two stories.

In 1993 a lady and her daughter flew to Guadalajara when I was there. They wanted to spend a week sightseeing, and knew I'd be on call if they had any problems. One evening, they joined me and what I term my Mexican family for supper at Sanborn's* restaurant. During the meal, the lady brought up safety in the local hotels.

My friend said, "We've heard of women being attacked in American hotels, but we cannot think of that here." He summed it up perfectly. The crime we put up with on a daily basis could not be envisioned in Mexico. Sadly, in the past twenty years, violent crimes of this nature have increased but still remain rare as compared to the risks in the U.S.A.

Several years ago an American youth was murdered in Matamoros, Mexico. It made all the news leads for several days. Paul Harvey pointed out that, despite this horrendous crime, an American stepping across the border was 50,000 times less likely to be murdered in Mexico than on our side of the border. It later came out that the ringleaders had been born in the United States.

With the exception of Mexico City and the border towns, Mexico is fairly safe. The people are outgoing, helpful and friendly to strangers. Courtesy is given and expected. There are reports that crime is increasing but I think of Mexico as being much like the United States was forty years ago. If you act like a decent person and treat people well, you'll be accepted and well liked. In a few days, you'll realize you're perfectly safe, even at midnight in most Mexican cities. You'll find yourself becoming less distrustful of strangers. Still, take the same precautions you would in America. If someone around you has drugs,

---

* Sanborn's Insurance and Sanborn's Restaurants are not part of the same company. Sanborn's restaurants have an upscale store and bookstore attached. Many years ago they were virtually the only reliable quality restaurants in Mexico. After a week or two of hard driving in remote areas, they were always a great treat.

is intoxicated or is doing something illegal, get away from the situation immediately.

The exception to my thinking might be the so-called narco-terrorist problem. I have freely traveled Mexico during this period without fear or concern. I liken this crime wave to the Al Capone era in Chicago. The mobster and police encounters made huge headlines, but 99 percent of the population was never in danger or even likely to see any of these crimes. That is what I have found in Mexico. There is almost warfare between the drug gangs and military or police but it rarely involves the general population.

The two kinds of people I am most cautious about in Mexico are other Americans and Mexicans who have spent time in our cities. You already know how to judge Americans. Because of cultural differences, it's more difficult to judge a Mexican, especially one who has been an immigrant. Mainly, watch to see if the person is interested in improving his English or finding out about your home state. If that's the case, the person is probably okay. If his or her primary questions are about what you have or where you're staying, be cautious.

Always use your common sense. It'll carry you further in a questionable situation than anything I can recommend. When I say Mexico is fairly safe, that doesn't mean you'll be okay if you get drunk in a brothel and offer to fight everyone. Like many myths concerning Mexico —from weather to everyday safety— international travel lends itself to misconceptions unless common sense is applied. Many people feel safest traveling with a large tour group. In nature, hungry sharks do better feeding on schools of fish rather than seeking one or two fish. With thieves and pickpockets. it's similar. They're going to frequent the most popular areas and feed on the schools of tourists. Put yourself in the crook's shoes and ask is it safer to pick a mark out of a crowd being herded along or take on an independent eighty-year-old woman carrying a cane?

Health

With my U.S. medical insurance, I pay twenty-two dollars for a prescription. Every thirty days I require a refill of the 50 mg. tablets and spend another twenty-two dollars. I recently crossed the border at Piedras Negras, Mexico and stopped at a pharmacy. They had the Mexican equivalent of my medicine, but only in 100 mg. tablets. I bought a bottle of 100 tablets for $12.90. I have to suffer through breaking one in half each day, but I did get roughly six months of medicine for a little over half what a one month supply costs at home. Not all drugs cost less than stateside but it is worth checking. (If you purchase pharmaceutical drugs in Mexico, you may be required to have a prescription to bring them back into the States.)

Ha! You thought I was going to talk about the Mexican two-step or other health problems one might encounter in Mexico. There are a few concerns and I'll address some. But I prefer to look at the more positive aspect of health and medicine in Mexico first.

For years, I bought my eyeglasses in Mexico as they were less expensive and offered in more styles. Most optometrist shops will give you an eye test free of charge and many could make your glasses the same day. With the advent of safety lenses, I've again started purchasing my glasses on this side of the border. However, glasses, like prescriptions and even dentistry, are options a tourist can take advantage of in Mexico.

It is important to understand many Mexican products don't face the same scrutiny and standards they do in the United States before they are marketed. There is little legal recourse if one picks a bad physician or buys a product that is not up to our standards. It is definitely a case of buyer beware. If the traveler understands the negatives and takes proper precautions, great savings can be gained in medical care. It's important to ask around to learn which physicians or dentists have a good reputation. Most American consulates have a list of approved physicians.

There are many fine physicians in Mexico. The medical schools in Guadalajara and Monterrey train physicians, including Americans who return to the States to practice. With equipment and technology, it seems Mexican medicine outside the urban centers can run about twenty years behind the U.S., although this gap is rapidly closing. Many Americans who retire to Mexico buy into their medical system and use local physicians and facilities, but some fly back to the States for major operations. Additionally, some drugs no longer marketed or that now require prescriptions in the States remain available in Mexico. As a child, my mother treated me for ear infections with glycerin but I can no longer purchase it in America. My solution is to bring a bottle back from Mexico every few years.

Now, let's return to Montezuma's revenge. While once a concern all over Mexico, water purification systems and public health have made it less so. However, for those with concerns or those who are traveling to remote areas, I will address the problem.

If you are on a short trip, you can probably avoid any intestinal discomfort by drinking bottled water and avoiding unwashed vegetables —especially leafy vegetables— and ice cubes. On a longer visit, a diarrheal intestinal ailment is more likely. Most advice says to try to tolerate it for two or three days using over-the-counter drugs. However, if the diarrhea is more severe with abdominal cramps and even nausea and/or fever or blood in the stool, then you should seek medical advice. I suggest discussing this with your physician before leaving. Paregoric and Kaomycin are available without a prescription in Mexican pharmacies. Lomotil is no longer recommended. For most people, their first encounter with traveler's diarrhea is of the minor variety. However, with a severe bout, you can truthfully lose all modesty as you pull off the road and head for the nearest cactus to hide behind. When that happens, catchy phrases like the Mexican trot suddenly become abundantly clear.

Before venturing into Mexico for a long stay, the latest Centers for Disease Control (CDC) advisories should be consulted. One problem is entering malarial areas. I suggest consulting your family physician before leaving to decide what malaria-preventive medicines you might consider. Many of these drugs can be purchased in Mexico without a prescription, but must be used as recommended.

Visitors should check their personal insurance policies to determine what additional coverage they might require while out of the country. There are companies that provide for emergency medical evacuation. Medjet, 1-800-527-7478, is one such organization. Their webpage is www.medjetassistance.com and is worth checking for related coverage(s), from health to travel.

Also, check the information provided by Jim La-Belle at http://www.mexconnect.com/articles/222-purchasing-insurance-for-mexico. It is my understanding the Mexican tourist auto insurance policy offered by Mexpro.com includes international air ambulance to the U.S. or Canada and covers both ilnness

8. A view easily found around many Mexican cities.

and vehicle accidents.

Additionally, Seven-Eleven stores in Mexico sell cards that provide a variety of insurance coverage when activated. Some of these seem very reasonable and others a bit high. My Mexican motorcycle amigos purchase the health insurance cards when they take trips out of their home areas. The purchase ensures if they have an accident away from home, they will be covered by private physicians and hospitals.

These are cursory recommendations for the typical traveler. For the motorcyclist using a combination bike, the remoteness of areas to be explored must be considered and planned for differently. There are areas where physicians, much less drugstores, are not available. Alternative methods of travel not easily obtained must be found if an injury occurs. Each rider should try to prepare for as many eventualities as possible before entering isolated regions. A first aid kit, a method to purify water and extra food must be packed. Climate and wildlife have to be taken into consideration. Additionally, the health of your bike becomes almost as important as plans for your personal health and safety.

Maps

I've come to the proverbial fork in the road more than once in Mexico. I've looked at my map and re-verified the road I'm on still isn't there, nor is the fork. Every time, I've flipped a coin and ended up taking a doggone interesting road.

Mexican cities now have American-style malls and local maps are available. If you're staying over a day in a Mexican city, the investment in a city map is worthwhile. The best traditionally obtained map of the country I've seen is from AAA. However, even with that one, not all roads are represented.

The Mexican government is expanding the highway system. My last motorcycle trips occurred years ago, but I've traveled all the highways since and the information I provide, with noted qualifications, is accurate as of 2015. However, nothing can be taken for certain for more than a few months in Mexico. For instance, I've ridden from Veracruz to Tampico perhaps fifty times. On one trip, almost thirty miles of the old road was gone and the new road went via villages I'd never heard of or seen. Additionally, the road entering a Mexican city can be altered by government choice, or rapid urbanization can actually change the outskirts from rural to city. In either case, the traveler will enter at a different spot, causing some confusion until a current map can be consulted and ones' bearing regained.

I travel Mexico in most instances without a map but do not recommend this for anyone else. On my first trips, there were no good maps. I've learned the highway changes while traveling and never knew there were half decent maps until 1993. In recent years, so many new highways have been constructed even I can't keep up.

In 2011, I traveled for a month with the person I consider the best Mexican mapmaker, "Mexico" Mike Nelson, http://www.mexicomike.com/. I have seen no better maps anywhere for the new traveler. I now purchase single maps of certain cities for information on the junctions and interchange. If you are new to traveling Mexico, I cannot overstress how highly I recommend Mike Nelson's maps.

An Overview of Mexican History

It was steam-engine hot as Tomás and I walked from Chichén Itzá to Chichén Viejo. The jungle swallowed us within a minute. My tee shirt was sopping but I was no worse off from the interior Yucatán heat than my Mayan buddy. The sounds of milling tourists and passing autos faded quicker than 007's invisible ink could have. The thick vegetation allowed only the odor and sounds of vibrant jungle. We skirted a small, black water cenote* following a stony animal track. I considered a swim to escape the oppressive heat.

After fifteen minutes, Tomás parted some vine-covered branches and we stepped into Chichén Viejo. My energy surged back as I scanned the barely touched site. Bigger than Chichén Itzá and with two larger pyramids, this was what the Maya call Old Chichén. We had the entire site to ourselves and I was completely rejuvenated. Carved blocks lay tumbled over the ground. Unreconstructed ancient buildings broke the huge field. We strolled through the grass, where I stooped to examine a stone carving here and

* A cenote is basically an underground water reservoir. Yucatán has underground rivers where sinkholes appear, exposing the water. This is one type of cenote.

there, until we reached...

I knelt and ran my palms across the narrow stone path. It wouldn't have impressed many people, but this was the first Mayan causeway I'd ever seen. Many believe they date back to 1500 B.C. I'd heard pre-Mayan shards have been found under some of the causeways. Archeologists have more than enough to puzzle out concerning the first glimpses of Maya civilization. I've been satisfied following the professional work on these early civilizations, despite questioning some conclusions, but some people aren't. Some romantics and spiritualists see the causeways as having once run to Atlantis, among other fanciful speculations.

The short summary of Mexican history I present won't amount to one-tenth of the proverbial "spit in the ocean." It's not meant to, and couldn't be comprehensive for any of the major parts of Mexican history. Instead, it's a brief outline. I'm hopeful the reader will be stimulated to further reading.

As a Western nation, Mexico was over 250 years old when we had our revolution. Construction on the giant cathedral in Morelia began 45 years before the pilgrims landed at Plymouth Rock. Before the conquest of Mexico, there were a multitude of advanced Indian civilizations going back thirty-five hundred years, and some argue six thousand years. Several of the world's largest pyramids are in Mexico. The largest city on earth is Mexico City, and the Guadalajara metropolitan area is possibly more populous than New York. So, when you tour Mexico, the land

The figures I provide for Mexican cities are often higher than official counts. A glance at one fifteen-year-old copy of a popular guide gives a Mexico City population of four million more than the official count produced ten years later. An explanation is more than this book can encompass. The figures I've provided are from common tour guides I trust; however, if you visit, you will probably decide I've still underestimated the actual population.

9. El Tajín near Papantla, Veracruz is the most Oriental appearing archaeological site in Mexico.

area may be smaller, but the depth of historical time dwarfs that of the United States. Understanding these essential facts and preparing for the differences in culture and customs will help provide the tourist a more rewarding trip.

A study of Mexican history reveals many popular perceptions are inaccurate. A few revisionists currently see the Conquest of Mexico as evil Europeans taking over the land and people. The truth is, the Aztecs were among the most bloodthirsty people to have ever built a nation. Subjugated peoples were forced to send relatives to the Aztecs for purposes of human sacrifice, and this wasn't the worst of their horrific practices. The Conquest was not a matter of one culture or race destroying another. It was a matter of a multitude of Indian tribes and civilizations allying with the Spanish to destroy the Aztec empire.

A second misconception concerning Mexico is the

so-called War of Texas Independence. The war actually started with Mexican citizens —both Anglo and Mexicans— demanding the Mexican government, under General Santa Anna, abide by the Mexican constitution. The Texas Declaration of Independence wasn't even written until Santa Anna had already surrounded the Alamo. The truth is, Texas would still be part of Mexico had a dictator not usurped power, and Texas was not the only part of Mexico to declare independence.

Mexico retains the remnants of many advanced Indian civilizations. The visitor can walk among ruins, in all stages of restoration, going back to the beginning of recorded history. Many scholars compare Mexico's Indian history to ancient Europe. Waves of savage and barbaric tribes from the North would invade. They'd conquer the civilization they found and later another civilization would arise. But the traveler uninterested in Indian history may find other aspects of Mexican history of more interest.

The Conquest of Mexico impacts the world to this day. The changes and alterations in the development of world history are easily discovered. However, the subtle impacts —such as the increase in new foods available for a hungry world— are rarely mentioned. For those familiar with Mexican geography and the

Santa Anna. Antonio Lopez de Santa Anna, is one of the most interesting figures of the 19th century. The American view, often limited to the War for Texas Independaence, shortchanges the scope of the man. Santa Anna began his military career fighting for the Spanish against Mexican Independence before switching sides in 1821. He eventually ruled Mexico numerous times. He's remembered for his inept generalship in Texas, but that's a deceiving picture. Santa Anna was instrumental in defeating the Spanish when they attempted to retake Mexico in 1829. In 1838, three years after his Texas losses, he defeated a French invasion force at Veracruz.

Indian civilizations, the conquest by Cortés seems utterly impossible, even with Monday morning quarterbacking. The Spanish conquerors were often cruel and ruthless. Their only real ace in the hole was the fact the Aztecs were worse. Whatever one thinks of the Conquistadors when reviewing the history, one quickly concludes they were true supermen.

After the conquest, Spain ruled Mexico for three centuries as private royal property. This period can be termed "colonial." The discovery of silver stimulated the settlement of parts of Mexico. Although it was a harsh time, today's visitor is rewarded with many magnificent European-style cities and structures.

As I glance over this thumbnail sketch of Mexican history, I realize how inadequate it is, but I'd soon have a history book instead of a touring book if I presented more than a glimpse. Again, I encourage the reader to look to more complete works on favorite aspects of history, warfare, archeology, sociology, and other topics concerning Mexico. It's worth the effort and an increased knowledge in any area will enhance the visit of anyone spending more than a few days in this wonderful country.

10. Mexico border crossing at Eagle Pass, Texas.

2. Entry into Mexico and Travel Basics

As part of your trip planning and once you are underway, you'll need to know the following information and procedures to make your travel in Mexico go smoothly.

Basic Requirements to Enter Mexico with a Vehicle

(This information applies if you are traveling more than twenty miles from the border, or past the check point to officially enter Mexico proper.)

You will need a tourist permit. There are two transactions, one for you and one for your vehicle. A passport is required to enter Mexico and the U.S. government also requires a passport to re-enter the States.

1. The title to your vehicle and registration are required. The title must be in your name.
    If there is a lien against it, you will also need permission from the lienholder to take the car to Mexico.
2. A passport is required as well as a driver's license, if you are bringing in a car. Make certain your passport is still valid.
3. If you are taking minors over the border, you

must have their birth certificates and a notarized affidavit from their parents or your spouse (if it is your child and you are traveling without your spouse), giving you permission to travel with the child.

4. You must have proof of insurance (see below).

5. A credit card must be used to pay the entry fee. It assures the Mexican government you have the assets to be able to leave their country and not become a burden. Not all cards are accepted, but MasterCard and Visa both work equally well.

6. Make photocopies of each document on the American side of the border. Already having photocopies saves time and local charges for copying. You are normally sent to the Banjercito kiosk in the same building to have your documents reviewed and a fee of about $27 USD charged to your credit card. You will get this back when you return the permit within the time frame allowed. (If you are a day late, you forfeit your deposit.)

   When you leave Mexico, make absolutely sure the officers at the border cancel your permit.

7. Crossing the border at a smaller city usually makes the process easier.

   - Initials on one set of papers versus names on another set can cause slight delays.
   - Entry requirements can change quickly. Double-check the requirements before leaving on your trip.

     There are several sites that can be consulted. One is: http://www.mexonline.com/mexcustoms.htm. Mexconnect.com is a web-magazine that should be consulted by any Mexican traveler. The latest updates on requirements can also be found there.

To apply ahead of time for your vehicle permit online, visit the Banjercito site at https://www. banjercito.com.mx/registroVehiculos/

Insurance Information

1. Your American insurance does not cover you in Mexico's interior.
2. Under Mexican law, you are guilty until proven innocent.
3. Even a minor accident can result in huge problems, especially if you're not properly insured. Since 2013, liability is required in case you are at fault in an accident, with liability limits for a fatality capped at about $300,000 USD. Make certain your policy covers you for this.
4. Insurance can be obtained at the border from Mexican vendors or from several companies located in America. There is a link for insurance at: http://www.mexonline.com/mexcustoms.htm and also at http://www.mexconnect.com/articles/222-purchasing-insurance-for-mexico .
5. Sanborn's (http://www.sanbornsinsurance.com/) is well known for Mexican insurance. Tel. 800-222-0158, or call information for the local number at most any border town. There are other insurance carriers that sometimes have better rates. Weigh the value of better rates with the Mexican contacts a company has.
6. If you have an accident in Mexico, many people advise abandoning the vehicle and escaping the country. Don't do this if you have insurance. I advise paying for a minor repair on the spot.
7. Legal Aid generally comes with most auto insurance policies. Ask for it when you buy your insurance; it costs very little and is invaluable

should you have an accident. In the case of an accident, the insurer will post bond for you and will provide you with legal counsel.

Do You Need to Speak Spanish to Tour Mexico?

It's possible to enjoy Mexico without knowing a single word of Spanish. However, any effort you put into learning a few words will enhance the amount of pleasure you derive from your journey. I am far from fluent in Spanish, and I probably sound like a functional idiot to the natives. Still, I try and people take more time with me because of my effort.

However, speaking Spanish certain ways can cause more hilarity among the natives than not speaking it or even butchering the language. I was in the tiny Zacatecas tourist office learning about the city and cutting a bit of fool with the student/clerks when an American couple entered.

They were snooty and gave me a disparaging look as they approached the desk. I guessed they were a couple of Midwestern college professors on a tour. I kept my mouth shut and observed. She was attractive, but they were far-out-of-place anywhere, except behind a desk correcting English lit papers or lost in a library stack.

It was obvious from their first words they'd memorized all of the Spanish language they could from a textbook. They held a five-minute conversation, which included speaking with each other in Spanish. They knew far more of the language than I did; but when they left, the college kids and I laughed until we rolled. These two dolts sounded like first graders reading "Dick saw Jane." There was not a single error in their speech, but it sounded like a Spanish 101 textbook being painfully pronounced to a Spanish 201 book.

11. Mexican friends enjoying a cup of coffee in Tapalpa, Jalisco.

So, a tad of Spanish, however imperfect, can be better than actually memorizing books or tapes. There are several important elements to learning and speaking Spanish. I'll touch on a few; but keep in mind I am providing what I've found helped me.

I tend to slur or mumble words when speaking English. This laziness harms me in Spanish as exact pronunciation is more important. You should take a Spanish-English dictionary on your trip. Look up the vowel pronunciations and learn them. They are the same letters we use, but pronounced differently. Natives have trouble deciphering our Spanish if we are not exact in pronouncing the vowels. This is helpful for someone like me. I'm forced to speak slower and put more emphasis on sounds.

Many people who think they speak no Spanish fail to realize how many words they actually know. We've learned *amigo, mucho, muchacho, adios, dinero, grande, cerveza, arriba, señor, señorita, gracias, por favor* and *matador,* to name just a few from television, cartoons and movies. *¿Sí? o ¿No?*

Next, if you glance at the language dictionary, you'll notice many cognates. Some of these are:

Cemento   Cement

Restaurante	Restaurant
Exactamente	Exactly
Fantástico	Fantastic
Construir	To construct

My advice for those who don't speak Spanish or haven't taken a class in a long time is to review and stick to the words and cognates you know. Learn to count to twenty in Spanish and slowly add words during your trip.

The few phrases I would memorize before leaving are:

¿Tiene usted?	Do you have?
Me llamo...	My name is...
Dame...	Give me...
¿Cuánto cuesta... ?	How much...
¿En qué dirección?	In what direction?
¿Dónde está el baño?	Where is the bathroom?
Perdóname	Excuse / forgive me
Sin lechuga	Without lettuce
¡Ayúdame!	Help me!

The first two can be used to get most things if you use hand signs and point. *¿Tiene usted pan?* Do you have bread? *Dame una Coca.* Give me a Coke. If you can't recall the word for bread or Coke, use the phrase and point to what you want. The last one is perhaps the most important. It can be used in a store or restaurant to obtain aid or, should you be drowning, it's definitely the phrase you want to use!

Money: The Peso

Peso means "weight" and is the name used for Mexico's money. I don't know what the exchange value of the dollar to the peso will be when you visit, but there are several things to keep in mind. I've been able to work and think successfully in the monetary units of about a dozen countries and have dealt with many difficult changes in the Mexican peso. The worst time was in 1993, with the peso at 3,020 to the dollar. The Mexican government threw tourists a confusing curve in monetary exchange; a new peso without the last three zeros was introduced while the old peso was still in circulation. Therefore, there were different currencies floating around within the same country. A 50-peso note could actually be many thousands of pesos, but there were also 50-peso notes, which were only 50 pesos. All someone can do under such circumstances is to slowly figure out what you have in terms of American and Mexican money. Throughout the month, not a single individual tried to take advantage of my confusion over the currency and my naiveté in understanding it.

I hope such a currency change won't occur during your visit. If it does, just go slowly when using your pesos and make certain you're getting the correct notes when exchanging dollars. Remember:

1. Pesos may seem like play money because there are so many to the dollar. They're not, and your budget will break quickly if they're treated that way.
2. Exchange your dollars at fifty or a hundred dollars a time. Historically, the American dollar tends to increase in value against the peso. At times, you will gain pesos with subsequent exchanges.
3. With the advent of ATMs, it is easier to move around with less cash and acquire pesos as needed.

4. I used to rely on traveler's checks and often took several thousand dollars in traveler's checks when traveling. In recent years, it has become increasingly difficult to exchange traveler's checks in Mexico, and I no longer recommend them.

If you don't get a fair exchange rate at a business, use a credit card. That assures you get a fair exchange at that day's values.

Accommodations

You'll notice in this guide I offer little price information and only mention a few hotels. There's a good reason for that. If you'll bear with me, I'll review my observations on lodging for tourists in Mexico over the past forty-five years. It's important to recognize I personally don't put a premium on lodging and look for clean, reasonable accommodations. The costs I mention are in U.S. dollars.

In the 1960s and '70s, Americans searched for a hotel with clean rooms. These rooms were typically spartan and featured large ceiling fans to provide cooling. The big question when renting such a room was, "*¿Tiene agua caliente?*," or "Does it have hot water?" (This is still a worthwhile question for cheaper hotels and in remote areas.) Then, the cost was generally two to five dollars a night. Sadly, most of those bargains are gone. However, within the last decade, I've stayed in clean hotels paying six dollars in the state of Chiapas, thirteen dollars a couple of blocks off the main square in Merida and eight dollars in downtown Papantla.

Because of the low cost of lodging, I could once vacation for six-weeks in Mexico for what two-weeks would cost in the United States. That changed in the mid 1980s. Mexico embarked on a hotel build-

12. Talk about bike security —in Aguascialientes, I parked outside the door to my hotel room.

ing boom. Many of the new hotels made most of our best hotels seem like places to house poor relatives. The comparative beauty has to be seen to be grasped. But it must be kept in mind a form of feudalism still predominates in the Mexican economy. When one realizes the majority of the labor in construction and staffing the hotels might receive about eight dollars for a long day's work, it's understandable. Many of these hotels are located on the main routes through Mexico and obviously aimed at American tourists and wealthy Mexicans. Unfortunately, these new hotels often charged close to American prices.

My middle-class Mexican friends teased me gently that we "rich" Americans had made it economically impossible to vacation in their own country. Fortunately, most of them knew this rich American couldn't afford month-long trips at the new prices.

They often put me up or aided me in finding reasonably-priced rooms.

A Mexican friend is a true friend and will often insist you stay with him. This is wonderful hospitality, but it can limit your activities. If you're lucky enough to have such amigos, it can be a delicate diplomatic situation convincing them to let you stay in a nearby hotel.

It's not uncommon to find hotels, bars and restaurants with so little business they couldn't survive in the United States. In the mid 1990s, the realities of the marketplace collided with the feudalistic aspect of Mexico concerning hotel prices. Many of these wonderful hotels, despite the financial advantages of low building and staffing costs, had to lower prices to attract customers. For this reason, I'm reluctant to list rates. They may change greatly within six months time. It's best to augment this guidebook with a yearly guidebook focusing on lodging. These will provide a list of the best-known quality hotels in every area of Mexico. They won't save you money, but are handy should you reach an area too late to search for a more affordable room.

Today, entering and exiting many Mexican cities, you'll find chain hotels and new smaller hotels, resembling U.S. motels. Many of these have excellent prices and are well kept. They should be considered, but keep in mind that walking is the way to go in most Mexican cities. I recommend searching for a hotel off the town's central plaza, often called the *plaza de armas, el jardín, el centro* or *el zócalo*. The costs are normally better, although many lack the amenities a chain or multi-star hotel might offer. On the other hand, you'll more than likely meet Mexicans and learn more about the culture and area than when staying at a hotel aimed specifically at passing motor-

13. Two buddies enjoying the square in Mérida.

ists. A motorcycle is certainly easier to scoot around on than a car, but generally a room near a downtown area puts one within easy walking distance for most needs. It's hard to go more than three blocks without passing pharmacies, restaurants, bakeries, *fruterías* and small stores.

Most hotels have their own parking areas. Guards are stationed at these lots or garages and make the traveler feel more secure about leaving his vehicle. For the motorcyclist, many inns allow a bike to be parked next to the room, if not actually in the room.

The word motel has a bad connotation in much of Mexico —as it once did in America— as a place for lowlifes and prostitutes. Near the border, in northern Mexico, "motel" may be used in our current sense of the word, and one can usually tell at a glance if it's a motel or a house of ill-repute. But the reputable meaning fades rapidly as one moves south.

Many cities and localities have their own fiestas. A fiesta can increase the number of visitors to a city and influence room prices and availability. Expect costs to be higher and fewer rooms available if you arrive at a town during fiesta. If you know your route and dates, check the towns you plan to visit to ensure you have a room, or even avoid them during a period of celebration.

Roads and Traffic

It's mid-afternoon and I'm cruising along at fifty miles per hour. The weather's superb, and my jacket makes the temperature perfect. It's an excellent, new, lonely road winding through long, gently-sloping hills, working themselves into the mountains ahead. I suddenly enter a half-mile slit cut through the dome of a hill. Sharp, beveled stone slants down on each side of the highway, but my immediate concern is the blue Volkswagen Beetle approaching in my rearview mirror. Mexican drivers normally pass a yard to the left, so I usually hold a spot about three-fourths of the way over in my lane. That position allows plenty of highway on my right should the passing driver not pull far enough to his left.

I judge the Beetle is going about sixty or seventy mph when my eye catches the cab of a red, Ford pick-up overtaking the Volks. All appears fine. The Volks is easing into the left lane to pass. I decide to hold my position to the last second before edging right, but events change quickly. The red truck roars around the Volks and their duet-like swing left has revealed an even faster blue Dana pickup pulling left to pass them both. I've been re-acclimated to Mexican driving. I don't panic, but ease to the right. Amazingly all three vehicles pass me at the same instant! Not a single one of them has broken speed or touched their brakes. I'm cussing —not at the driving, but at the fact I wasn't filming the event.

In 1996, I sold a humor article, "Mexican Road Rules" to *Great Outdoors Recreation Pages,* or GORP (http://gorp.away.com/gorp/location/latamer/mexico/

roadrule.htm), an Internet travel magazine. They used many of my observations in an article that has remained popular. Since then, several Mexico-related web sites have used parts of the article, often introducing their interpretations into the body of the work. These observations were very accurate pre-1995 Mexico and truth in most of the points lingers into today's Mexico. I've updated the original article and included it below.

Mexican Road Rules

"Twenty-Five Tips for Americans Driving in Mexico"

As you leave the American border and enter Mexican traffic, expect shock and awe as seven lanes of traffic form at 45 mph on a road designed for three. Despite the differences in traffic rules, you'll soon become accustomed to hesitating at a light or stop sign for a second, then shooting across the intersection. You'll take pedestrians and vendors in stride as you whirl through the morass of traffic and people. You'll adjust to passing horse-drawn wagons or pausing as cattle cross a city street. The following twenty-five tips on Mexican roads and driving may make you smile; but beware. At some point during your trip, you'll adjust and may even come to prefer many of the Mexican highway rules and customs.

1. Many travelers find the Mexican road system to be a succession of potholes with a patch of cement or asphalt thrown sporadically about. Others argue the Mexican Highway department has large elephants wade through the asphalt before it's fully cool. Unfortunately, those ideas become reasonable, and you better drive watching for the "mother of all potholes" at all times.

2. Just because you spent three hours over a leisurely meal that would have taken twenty minutes in the United States, the Mexican you ate with doesn't take all parts of life as if there was no hurry. That same person with whom you talked, joked and sipped an extra glass of wine before enjoying two, last-minute cups of coffee will undergo an extraordinary metamorphosis after he or she leaves the restaurant and slips into the driver's seat. From the moment the key turns the ignition, that person with seemingly unlimited time doesn't have a second to lose. Traffic lights and stop signs are suddenly obstacles to be overcome. Posted speed limits mean nothing. It's as if he has entered the most important race ever run, and not until he reaches his destination will he again assume a sane existence.

3. Mexico has many toll roads. The fee is based on what a member of the Rockefeller family could afford. One of the few toll roads worth the cost is between Juárez and Chihuahua. This particular road is valuable because it takes you quickly through roasting desert. Since there is no good alternative road, you may as well pay with a smile. Other toll roads that might be worth their cost are those through Mexico City and Arco Norte. Toll roads, or *cuotas,* are the only way to avoid bad highways. Still, an occasional pothole will appear out of nowhere, meaning the driver better stay alert. Of course, it's easier to watch for potholes on the toll roads as they have been constructed in areas devoid of scenery.

4. Yes, Martha, you did see that! We were sitting in the left-hand lane waiting for the light to change so we could turn left. Yes, two cars to our right turned left in front of us as the light changed so

14. Enjoying coffee in rural Tabasco during my second trip.

they could beat the three lanes of traffic that sped across from the other direction.

5. Beware! You're adjusting. You just nosed out a compact car for a superior position in traffic.

6. Ahah! You've somehow survived and been ejected from your first *glorieta,* the Mexican version of a traffic circle. Why aren't these Mexicans putting men on the moon? How can eight —or was it thirteen— lanes pour into a giant circle, with several lanes running through the circle, several lanes flowing under the circle and traffic lights somehow signaling some areas, with cars speeding through, crossing lanes, entering, exiting and seemingly never stopping? You'll enter the next six or seven *glorietas* filled with trepidation. Then you'll begin to anticipate the challenge.

7. What about the bumps in the road called "*topes*?" Remember them when approaching villages! These speed breakers are often dangerously high, to the point a car can overturn by hitting them

too fast. They may be inconvenient, but they're cheaper than hiring highway patrol officers.

8. Martha, you can get up from the floorboard now. It's okay! Yes, we were driving at 45 mph when the pickup truck on our right turned left in front of us! No, I don't know why we didn't wreck. I closed my eyes.

9. Open road driving between Mexican cities differs from the U.S. The speed limits are posted, but there is no highway patrol. You're on the honor system!

10. Beware! You're adjusting too well. You just nosed an eighteen-wheeler out for a superior position in traffic.

11. The road is clearly marked, three lanes each way. Don't let it worry you that your side has turned into five lanes. There's still room for a motorbike, but you might feel sorry for the three opposite lanes. They've turned into six lanes and a donkey cart has just edged off the sidewalk in front of them.

12. A tourist will be constantly impressed by the honesty of the Mexican people, except at some gas stations. Years ago, virtually every attendant and owner was helpful and honest, but times have changed. An American should watch the attendants where inexperienced North Americans purchase gas. The pump indicators can be confusing, and some attendants will overcharge if they have the opportunity. Americans visiting by car for the first time should fill up more often than is necessary. When the gauge reads half-empty, know more or less how many gallons it will take to top off the tank. Count out enough pesos for the gallons necessary and specifically tell the attendant, "I want this much, only." Continue this practice

15. Oxxo, a typical Mexican convenience store, in Progreso, Yucatán. Such stores started appearing in the 1980s.

until you become accustomed to the pumps and numbers. It will prevent small thefts.

13. Where do I park? How does one know? The Mexican uses logic and it works. Try it yourself. Park where you want, but be darn sure a large bus can pass. It's a good idea to push outside mirrors flat against the car.

14. Car stalled on a lonely road with no shoulder? Don't worry! Just leave it on the road until you get help. Everyone drives aware someone might be stalled so you're probably safe.

15. Beware! Mexican road rules and traffic etiquette are starting to make sense. You've enjoyed a sense of accomplishment and are beginning to realize your true driving skills. In the States, you would have never squeezed between a city bus and an eighteen-wheeler so you could be the first person to pass the Volkswagen Beetle.

16. Worried about deer where you live? In Mexico, you'd better worry about more than Bambi. Learn to drive defensively. In the cities, every kind of pedestrian, bicycle, pushcart and horse cart will vie for a space on the road. In the country, it's worse. Deer pale in comparison to worrying about freely roaming cows, horses and donkeys.

17. You're cruising along, doing about fifty through the city, secure in an outside lane of four going one way. Without warning, your lane ends. You slam on brakes, curse and stare in amazement. No sweat. It'll happen three or four times. Then, during your next encounter with a dead end and without a second thought, you'll merge with other traffic.

18. "All roads lead to Rome" should be changed to "...Mexico City." The Romans didn't have a clue when they coined that expression, but Mexico City knows how to make it true. In Mexico, Mexico City is referred to as just Mexico. The word means more the city than the country. At virtually every sign signaling direction, there is also one reading Mexico. You can be going directly east, west, north or south away from Mexico City and signs will read "(to) Mexico." Ironically, less than a half mile from one American border crossing is a sign saying "(to) U.S. Border and Mexico."

Until recently, the only easy way to avoid driving through Mexico City was to stay on the east or west coast highway and never venture inland. On five occasions, before Arco Norte, I've tried to cross central Mexico without going through Mexico City. Each time, I memorized the small roads and towns on the route. One time I actually made it. It took an extra day and a half to avoid the additional sixty to ninety miles that would have taken me through Mexico City.

19. So, the local policeman stopped you for some minor infraction. He wants to give you a ticket and take your license until you come to the station and pay the thirty-dollar fine. You have a problem, but you don't have to pay the fine. The question is, can you get off with the two-dollar bribe the average Mexican would pay to escape the fine

16. Taking a break a hundred miles from Oaxaca.

or will you end up paying five or six dollars? It's time to test your bargaining skills and to selectively use less Spanish than you know. But even a six-dollar bribe is preferable to the thirty-dollar inconvenience.

20. Beware! You just made a middle lane in moving two-way traffic so you could get around a slow truck. Definitely insanity, but you're beginning to wish the United States would adopt some of these traffic rules.

21. Get over that American male hang-up about asking for directions. Mexican cities are crowded and fast moving. You won't see every sign, and many won't correspond to the map or route you've planned. Stop and ask! The one time I managed to avoid Mexico City, the roads on the map didn't correspond to reality. I had to stop and ask directions at virtually every intersection.

22. See those little crosses beside the curves in the highway? That's where someone didn't heed the

warning signs and died. When you see warning signs, take note.

23. Mexicans claim they have a lower auto accident rate than the United States. That's probably true. Everyone drives defensively at all times.

24. What do you do in heavy speeding traffic when you're cut off? Hit your brakes, of course! Oh no, not in Mexico. In some areas, there are signs instructing you to use your horn, not your brakes.

25. Beware, too late! Your driving attitude is now Mexican. The truck without lights you just ran up on during a dark night didn't faze you. You're responsible for yourself on the road, and you enjoy the challenge.

Bonus rule: You've been prepared for almost everything you might encounter in Mexico. Now, you're ready for Mexico City —if anyone can ever be prepared to drive in Mexico City! Take all the above rules you find fault with and multiply them by a factor of twenty. Even Mexicans talk about the bad driving in Mexico City. Nothing can prepare you for huge buses sandwiching you or the volume of cars speeding past. Literally expect anything possible with a vehicle to occur in the world's largest city.

There's an element of truth in each of these tips. At first, Mexican traffic will scare the beejeebees out of you. A friend, who recently made his first trip into Mexico with me, termed it "combat driving." His statement is a great summarization. Yet very quickly, many of their driving customs begin to make perfect sense. Just relax and enjoy yourself. Every one of those other drivers is as aware and watchful of you as you are of them.

* * * * *

17. Not a first class bus, but your goat rodes free in rural 1970s Campeche.

Overall, the roads in Mexico are terrible. If more than a few months have passed, the information someone gives you about a highway's condition is often unreliable. There is no weight limit on trucks, so the roads are constantly under repair. A great road six months ago can be rubble today, and a bad road in mint condition. The only exceptions are toll roads. But as previously mentioned, they're expensive and you see little of the country. Mexico is definitely improving its highways, but expect the worst gravel or dirt lane you've encountered in the United States to surpass some sections of Mexican highways.

Driving conditions involve far more than the highways. Huge potholes and cracked, broken and strangely melted surfaces characterize Mexican roads. Never let several miles of smooth pavement lull you into feeling secure. As soon as you do, a pothole will catch you.

In the country, you won't see police patrols. This means most people drive in excess of eighty mph; but God help you if you hit a *tope*, (a speed bump) a *vado*, (a dip in the road for water runoff) or a large pothole going over fifty. Occasional a hole can literally swallow your tire. Much of the land is open range. Mules, horses, donkeys and cattle stray onto the roads. Most roads lack shoulders and it's common for cars and trucks to be stalled or parked in your lane. On long straight stretches, you don't realize parked vehicles aren't moving until you're almost on top of them. As you enter some towns, there will be a wrecked vehicle mounted on a flatbed by the welcome sign. It's the Mexican way of saying, "This will occur if you don't follow the honor system."

Night Travel

I'd ridden far too long that day and foolishly entered Toluca well after dark. My budget dictated a reasonable hotel, but I didn't know where a hotel was, only that I was lost. I cruised around until spotting an expensive hotel. I wasn't spending a hundred and twenty-five bucks for a room. The clerk, however, directed me to an affordable hotel.

It felt great seeing the beckoning sign. I could get a hot meal and some coffee. At least that's what I thought until I rode by and couldn't find the entrance. I had to go five blocks before finding a spot to turn around. My next three passes were equally futile. Finally, I pulled off, waited for lulls in traffic and inched along until I could spot a break in the curb that allowed access. This hotel was the equivalent of the first and eighty-five dollars cheaper.

It is not a good idea to travel after dark. Many vehicles lack taillights. The traffic problems I've already mentioned are compounded at night. Unfortunately, this is the one safety rule I break most often and always kick myself for doing so. I'm easily dis-

18. A road scene in Tabasco in the early 1970s.

tracted. I'll plan correctly for a jaunt between cities, but run into something interesting on the way and end up lollygagging too long. The next thing I know, I'm foolishly riding in the dark.

Night problems in the cities often result from different traffic flow and patterns than one might expect. Mexican cities are more ancient than ours, and many roadways are narrower or split in ways not immediately obvious to the American mind. A road marked for three lanes will carry as many lanes of traffic as can be squeezed together. In the dark, your mind is more focused on your safety than on reading street signs. Needless to say, we gringos should carry defensive driving to new heights at night and especially while on a motorcycle.

Section II

From an Old Dream to Reality

19. Leaving Columbia, South Carolina for Mexico, June 1971.

3. A New Bike and Reflections

Leaving Victoria, Mexico, heading south, the weather in June 1971 was perfect for a bike trip. My only problem was nervousness as I rode farther from my country and the people who spoke my language. The air blew crisp and cool in the bright sun on the lonely road. I topped the mountain crests surrounding Victoria and began my descent. Concerned about obtaining gas in Mexico, I cut the motor to glide. I felt as free and easy as the eagles soaring effortlessly above me as I scanned the huge empty valleys I had yet to cross. Silence reigned as I rounded curves, occasionally braking lightly, while gravity pulled me toward the valley floor. Twenty-seven miles later, I shifted into fourth gear and restarted my engine. Had I really coasted that far? I know I did but, years later, the length leads me to question my own memory.

Fast forward twenty-one years when I found, along with the children's Christmas presents, my wife had surprised me with a screaming red Honda 250 Nighthawk. Although I was thrilled, apprehensive thoughts and vivid memories flashed through my mind. Was I too old to ride? I hadn't touched a bike in years. What about my occasional back problems, stamina and reaction time at my age?

"Thanks, but can we afford a motorcycle?" I asked. No two ways about it, I was scared of the motorcycle.

My wife sensed it immediately.

"We can take it back," she said, giving me an out.

"No way!" I was nervous, but I'd have wanted the motorcycle if I'd been seventy-five. Years earlier, I had bought a red Honda SL 175 and rode it from Columbia, South Carolina, to Yucatán, Mexico, and back. The ten thousand mile, two-month plus trip had been one of the great adventures of my life. I'd recalled that trip many times, always hoping to someday repeat it.

After Christmas, I slowly re-acclimated myself to riding a motorcycle. I spent time learning to lean into curves again, grasping every aspect of the bike's capabilities, asking myself probing questions as I rode. When I was younger, was I as aware of the possibility of cars pulling out? Was I as cautious coming to stops? Did I fear the motorcycle at high speeds? It was hard to remember from twenty-plus years earlier. I didn't recall the wind affecting me before, but now I felt it influencing the bike's course.

On that first trip to Mexico, I often thought of myself akin to the wild Hunnish warriors on their small sturdy horses. They rode for weeks, sometimes never dismounting. They were a part of their horses and helpless without them. The bike had become a part of me as I almost lived on it for two solid months.

I had been alone in a foreign nation. No friends and family, and I didn't speak the language. My only way home was my bike, which I rode day after day, never, letting it out of sight, even taking it into hotel rooms. What was wrong now? Why wasn't I becoming a part of this bike as I had the other?

I only sporadically mounted the 250 Nighthawk. Each short ride brought more of my ability and confidence back. The idea of a longer trip when the weather was better —maybe to the Outer Banks, the

Smokies and Blue Ridge Parkway, or perhaps even a thousand miles, as far as Key West— popped into my mind each time I rode. All were great trips for a biker but from somewhere deep within, questions loomed and an old urge tugged. Am I still brave or tough enough to take Mexico alone on a bike? Will my body and mind hold up to the rigors of such a quest? For many years I had wanted to repeat that trip, perhaps even go further. Now was the time to do it or quit fooling myself.

My first opportunity to travel in Mexico had come unexpectedly. I had quit construction work and returned to college as a married student. Anthropology students were offered twelve hours credit for independent study in Mexico. Despite struggling financially, my wife agreed it was a worthwhile opportunity. I wrote a proposal to study ancient Indian ruins and the school approved. The bike cost approximately $800 and the entire trip cost $290 for food, gas and lodging. I even brought back a few presents on that astronomical budget, having eaten breads and fruits at remote villages at almost no cost. People often invited me to stay in their homes. My wife's graciousness was rewarded as I discovered the beauty and safety of Mexico. In subsequent years, we've vacationed there almost yearly. Yet, despite the many visits and having more money, none of those trips provided the freedom and adventure of that first, long bike ride.

In 1971, very basic, clean hotel rooms were three to five American dollars. Today, most hotels are more modern and with a bit of searching can be found in the $30 to $50 range. I realized there would be changes besides cost. At almost fifty years of age, I wondered if I would be as welcome in small villages as I had been as a younger man. Perhaps people would still accept a lone biker as someone interesting, a vagabond adventurer with intriguing human interest stories regardless of age. I wanted to answer those questions about the older me, my spirit of adventure and doubts. I wanted to absorb the changes in Mexico from the back of a motorcycle on a slow ride.

In 1971, I'd never driven a motorcycle. I bought one and rode around for 521 miles. That was the extent of my experience before I left to explore Mexico. I had 969 miles on this second bike when I crossed the border. At times, when contemplating the second trip, the reckless abandonment of a teenager again captured my soul. In 1971, the people at the Honda shop in Monroe, Louisiana, stayed open late to give the bike a thorough check-up once they knew my destination. I received the same excellent service again in Texas before crossing the border. Preparing to leave, I hoped the Honda service people would still be as skillful and helpful. I had one advantage this time. Previously, Mexico had its own national motorcycle company, Islo. There were no imports, American or Japanese, much less Honda service centers. My little combination SL 175 was considered a huge bike in Mexico. People often gathered to admire the "large" bike with, unbelievably, two cylinders. This trip, I knew there were Honda shops, among an assortment of other motorcycle shops, and that was reassuring. I've never been a great mechanic.

When I crossed the border in '71, at Brownsville, Texas into Matamoros, Mexico, I was hassled by the border guard. I spoke no Spanish and didn't know if I would be allowed to enter. The guard insisted I buy Mexican highway insurance. Paying his price would have broken my budget and I'd have to abandon my trip. I stood frustrated, not knowing what to do, when a young woman appeared. She was learning English

20. Despite the jungle-shrouded pyramid in the distance, this is not a place where you want to break down in the Yucatán peninsula.

and helped me by reminding the guard, "A cyclist doesn't need insurance." (The motorcyclist must have insurance today.)

The man shrugged and stamped my visa. I talked with the auburn-haired young woman for thirty minutes. For the first time, I realized how little Mexicans know about the United States and how little I knew about them. I was surprised at her hair color and fair skin. She was curious about South Carolina and its location. She knew of Texas, California and New York. That is the extent of what most Mexicans know of the United States; but the young woman will always be in my memory for her assistance, graciousness and friendliness.

At the end of May 1993, I knew I'd take a second, long trip. More importantly, I was now taking curves at 45 mph. Only a month earlier, I'd felt shaky at 25 mph. The motorcycle was gradually becoming a part of me. Still, the realization I was going brought a new set of fears, problems, memories and tasks. I was no longer a carefree youth. I needed to foresee every possibility, recall the mistakes I made on the first motorcycle trip and utilize what I had learned then and in subsequent trips. A proper checklist had to be prepared and everything packed to perfection to maximize my storage space.

Undoubtedly, the border guards would hassle me again, as is the Mexican routine. Every paper had to be in order. I discovered a credit card is required instead of two hundred dollars cash, as had once been the case. Past experience taught it was best to have two or more of the required items and still be prepared to pay a small bribe (*mordida*) for entry. This "tip" is frowned on today but was once customary due to the low wages the guards receive. When supervision is relaxed, the *mordida* is an accepted part of the culture and only a dollar or two are necessary.

There are times when a guard will demand too much. If you're in an area where there are other crossings nearby, you can tell a dishonest guard to forget it and travel to another. If you don't have that opportunity, you can beat a greedy guard at his game by playing dumb and out-waiting him. You will invariably be allowed through, but it takes patience. In these instances by the time you cross, you probably won't reach your first planned destination before nightfall.

In recent years the government has tried to end *mordidas*. I have noticed a drop in demand. The traveler should keep both views in mind and less readily volunteer a dollar or two. Watch the officer and determine if he's hinting for a tip.

I reread the Honda manual while preparing to leave. The instructions brought back fascinating memories of being broken down beside a jungle clearing in the Yucatán Peninsula. The last rays of light were falling and I was nearly a hundred miles from the nearest town with electricity. The jungle closed over the road. Bird and animal sounds echoed as night slammed over the earth. I'd finished reading the manual, but had to fumble in the dark, listening to jaguars roar, as I'd neglected to pack a flashlight. I'd also failed to bring extra fuses, but managed to directly link the correct wires and crank the bike. The lack of fuses would later cost me, but I escaped spending a long night in the jungle without any preparation.

The new repair manual was still as clear as it had been years earlier. All of the adjustments, methods to make minor repairs and preventive maintenance information were explained in easily understood language. I appreciated its clarity. On my first trip, I'd done my own work, which was quite an undertaking for someone with limited mechanical experience. The little manual had saved me several times, and I knew it would assist me again if it were necessary.

Two Saturdays before leaving, it was time to mount the saddlebags. They looked awfully flimsy and small. My dismay increased by the moment as I assembled and mounted them on the bike. They had the worst directions I'd ever encountered. Korean or Japanese script with good pictures would have been superior. After spending an hour more than should have been necessary, I was still dissatisfied and left with questions concerning their value. The snap buttons read, "lift on spot," but no matter how I tried, they wouldn't unsnap and only closed with great difficulty. I rode to the Honda shop and asked the salesman if he knew the trick to opening the little silver buttons. After several tries he gave up, afraid he would pull the rivet through the strap. He promised he would call someone to see if they knew the secret. Only time and travel would tell if the bags were better than their assembly directions, but I hated leaving with such doubts about some of my equipment. The purchase of an old army pack supplemented the bags and allowed the extra storage I needed.

With nine days to go, I took my longest ride, a ninety-five mile round trip. I left at 5:00 p.m., and traveled at 65 mph most of the way. The temperature was 100 degrees Fahrenheit. I thought I recalled how hot the road can get, but I'd been fooling myself. Oven-like heat bounced off the road, baking me. The speed provided little relief.

I returned at 11:00 p.m. The wind was up. I rode nervously and there was now no doubt: strong currents of air definitely affected this bike more than I liked. For the first time, I doubted the bike's ability. I debated trading for a larger bike, but decided I'd ride at slower speeds in windy conditions. That would work fine in Mexico, as I planned on an easy ride. However, in the States I wanted to maximize speed. I'd have to find out if the old Honda SL 175 had been heavier or built with a lower center of gravity than this 250. I was now sure the difference was in the bike and not in the older rider.

Six days before I left, doubts still plagued me. I had everything ready, except I couldn't find an old-style army canteen. (The kind that sweats through cloth and keeps water cool is a must during the long stretches of highways. Torrid heat and high winds can dehydrate a rider in a matter of hours.) Should I go? What if I were involved in a traffic accident? What if my wife and kids needed something while I was away? Could I come up with a perfect excuse to back out? I woke up with such thoughts. I felt real fear for the first time. There was no reason for backing out. So why was I filled with questions, remorse and concern? Was it my young sons who had been helping me prepare? Was I homesick before I left? I'd go, but I was searching for an excuse even as the urge for adventure tugged me forward. Only a real emergency would stop me, and I hoped one didn't occur.

At almost the last minute, I found I had to go to Santa Fe, New Mexico on business before entering Mexico. After discussions with friends, I decided to truck the bike to the border. I didn't like the idea of trucking a bike even part of the way, but a tropical storm had just dropped ten inches of rain in Texas and was moving east. The bad southeastern weather clinched my decision. Riding the bike via Santa Fe would be slower and mean losing five days for Mexican travel. I could store the truck in El Paso, Texas and enter from there.

"Gee Dad, you're really going!" It was time to leave and my oldest son's words revealed for the first time my sons think their dad is too old for such trips. Now I had to go, no matter what self-doubts bedeviled me. Although his words made leaving more difficult, I couldn't have my boys thinking this trip was suddenly too tough to tackle. It felt exhilarating to start despite the sadness of leaving for I knew how a thirteen- and an eight-year-old see their dad.

21. Despite a gloomy sky, there are some breaks you'd like to last longer. I enjoyed watching the fishermen on Lake Yuriria outside Morelia.

4. South to Chihuahua

The drive west was frustrating. It kept me off the bike and the beginning of my real trip. Crossing Arkansas was a surprise. I hadn't expected substandard roads until I entered Mexico. Bumping along, one thought kept banging into my mind —I hope whoever built those roads got a good kickback. It was disgraceful if this construction was the best they could do.

At 9 a.m. June 24th, I stored my truck in El Paso, Texas, and finally left for the border. My body tingled with energy and enthusiasm as I cruised down Montana Avenue and pulled into the local bank. Strolling up to the cashier, I changed a hundred dollars to pesos. I always change my first hundred dollars on this side of the border so I know the exchange rate will be accurate. It's an old habit formed before money exchange houses were common in Mexico, but a practice I continue.

Leaving the bank with a bundle of foreign bills, I cruised twelve blocks and stopped at Sanborn's Insurance office. The cost for motorcycle liability insurance for a thirty-day trip was more than I liked. Plus, there was no longer a refund if you leave Mexico early. With such strict policies, I wondered if I should have purchased insurance from a local company or at the border itself. However, that was a fleeting thought, as I had long used and been satisfied with Sanborn's. I got their receptionist to notarize a statement swearing I was born in the United States. I, who knew better, had forgotten my birth certificate. The sworn statement was a last minute safety valve.

I finally crossed the international bridge from El Paso into Juárez, Mexico. The traffic rules changed as my bike climbed the bridge. Extra lanes started forming in an unorganized mass moving toward the border station. The entry point has improved for tourists in recent years, but is still difficult. I find it comparable with registration for classes at a major university before computerization. There are several buildings and offices for entry. Unfortunately, there's not a single sign in English to help an American decipher the maze. I went to five wrong places until trial and error led me to the correct desk.

I would provide the proper steps to help other visitors, but I sometimes feel the order of entry changes throughout the day and depends on a bureaucrat getting tired of watching a frustrated gringo try to find the correct point. That's not true, of course, and once I understood the order of progression, the entire process took twenty minutes. Toward the end, I hit one of those points that made me question if I wanted to enter Mexico and leave my tourist dollars. A small fee, as described previously, is required to enter the country. It has to be paid on a MasterCard and they keep a photocopy. I think they would make adjustments if someone lacked a MasterCard, but I suggest anyone visiting have one or call the Mexican embassy in Washington, D.C., to find out what can replace it. I recommend a MasterCard be brought regardless of it being required. It is widely accepted and, in an emergency, would provide funds to exit the country.

The final confusion began when a young woman took five other travelers and me to the parking lot to paste metallic stickers on our vehicles. I'd parked

22. A curious boy like this one in La Quemada, Zacatecas, can show up anywhere.

my bike in the wrong lot. It sat twenty yards on the other side of a chain link fence. The young woman wasn't allowed to enter that part of the embarkation compound, and didn't want me to retrieve the bike by riding through the gate in front of us. She and the other tourists waited while I ignored the open gate and walked over, up and back a block to reach my motorcycle and return to the correct lot.

Entering Juárez traffic, fear and shock nearly overcame me as seven lanes of traffic jammed together on a road designed for three. Yet, I expected it. Crossing Juárez, I recalled the difference in traffic rules. I adjusted my speed passing a horse drawn wagon.

What about the bumps in the road called *topes*? I've got to remember them as I approach villages. They're often dangerously high and easy to forget about. Come on, go slow. It'll all come back, I reminded myself. Today, just enjoy the sights and smells of humanity.

The entry was easier than I expected. I was in an upbeat mood as I encountered the obstacles and differences in driving. The road was more clearly marked than I'd ever seen. It would take a little while to get used to the different placement of street lights and traffic signs (often high and far to the left), but it would all come together. But, brother is it reassuring to know you're at least on the right road!

Leaving El Paso, I gained a new concern. The area had been gripped in a heat wave. Today's expected high was 105. When visiting Mexico you must cross monotonous, hot desert first. All that crossed my mind was, I'm going due south, and it's going to be far hotter than El Paso's 105 until I reach the mountains.

About thirty miles south of Juárez, I hit the last checkpoint and spent twenty minutes talking with the guards about motorcycling Mexico. Five miles later, I stopped at the dunes to enjoy a drink of water, admire the absolutely barren sandscape and give thanks the road didn't pass directly through the Great Chihuahuan desert. I tilted my canteen for a healthy swig. A hot liquid with a foul, synthetic flavor flooded my mouth. I spit the polluted water on the parched sand almost as quickly as it entered my mouth. The old metal Army canteens always provided the taste of cool, refreshing water, but not this generic plastic version. I hoped the boys serving in our country's military didn't have to use plastic or polyurethane canteens. My first taste from it would be my last.

After the dunes, I began enjoying the sights and sounds of Mexico. Nowhere else can a motorcyclist feel freer than on the long, lonely highways between Mexican cities. The heat becomes bearable as adventure fills the traveler. Cruising along the barren land, I reflected on my first encounter with the people, and how different it would be now.

Pemex gas stations, owned by the Mexican National Oil Company, are rarely more than fifty miles apart. On the first trip, people falsely warned me the stations were a hundred miles apart, and to never pass one without filling up. I had no such worry this trip, but I couldn't help recalling that first trip.

23. Rural Northern Mexico in the 1970s.

About forty miles into Mexico, I spotted a sign indicating a little town four kilometers to the left. Worried about gas, I decided to search for a station. I hit the town and slowly rumbled over the cobblestones. What was going on along the two-storied street? I uneasily looked right and left as people poured out of their businesses and homes. Men were holding children on their shoulders while barefooted little boys in colorful, unbuttoned shirts ran into the street and jogged beside me. Everywhere I looked, people were pointing at me.

Was it my helmet? Did they hate Americans? Were they going to attack me? What if some of the horror stories about American treatment in other nations were true? At the end of the three-block street, the crowd closed in. I couldn't go forward. No one touched the motorcycle or me, but they stared and talked among themselves. What am I doing here, I wondered?

Obviously, all these small, brown people speaking

so rapidly were deciding what to do to me. Finally, a man shook my hand and gestured for me to dismount and step forward. With the few words of Spanish I knew (most of which came from watching "The Cisco Kid") and observing their actions, I figured out what was going on. I was being introduced and welcomed by the mayor, or some such official, in an impromptu ceremony. A translator stepped forward. He knew less English than I did Spanish, but he impressed the town's people with his worldliness as he garbled loudly, "Thank you very much. You American, me Mexican. Good night. In Texas, I wetback."

I eventually determined the man had been an illegal alien working on a Texas farm years earlier. Although less than sixty miles from the United States border, the townspeople had never seen a North American and were celebrating my arrival. The men and women stroked the bike, and I allowed the children to sit on the "monster machine." I shook hands all around and left, still without gas, waving goodbye to the friendly crowd. I later stopped at a place saying "Gas," only to learn that sign meant butane, not gasoline. I finally found a Pemex station and discovered what their gas stations look like.

It was time to quit musing. I handled strange circumstances well in my younger years, but hoped this time I wouldn't encounter a situation I didn't understand. My bike flew through the sand and mesquite until a scorching headwind hit me. The heat wasn't a problem, but entering the flat, open land, I couldn't hold my speed with the blowing wind. The Nighthawk 250 wasn't aerodynamically sound. Four times from the right and once from the left, the bike felt like it was going to blow out from under me, as if the gusts were trying to flip the bike from the bottom instead of blowing me over from the top. It was a queasy feeling,

24. A typical roadside view in Northern Mexico.

moving at fifty-plus mph and thinking the wheels were about to flip out from under the bike.

Serious questions now loomed. The bike definitely performed poorly in windy conditions. It was the perfect excuse to stop. I moved slower and slower as the wind pressed against me. Could I continue or would it be too dangerous? It was a difficult decision. My questions and doubts were no longer about my ability and age. I was certain I had a bike that was dangerous to operate in strong gusts. It was a legitimate reason to stop. However, if I were careful, the bike would make it. I decided to continue and would creep along if the wind gained any force. I came upon a slow moving truck. Passing at 50 mph the wind shear almost caused me to swerve back into the truck's path. I could slow down and make it in this part of Mexico, but I wondered what the wind would do in the high mountains.

The little bit of traffic let up as quickly as it had come. I was again alone in scrub, semi-desert country. At forty-five mph, I was enjoying the small hills and dips. Thirty yards to my right, a rock-strewn dirt road paralleled the highway. Out of the brush a dilapidated brown ranch wagon appeared racing along behind four spirited mules. Up and down, they bounced over their stony lane. I followed the mule-driven wagon for a mile, barely believing I was seeing four working cowboys hightailing it somewhere. They had the same equipment as our nineteenth century cowboys. But their speed was much greater than I could have imagined.

Twice, I sped ahead to take pictures, only to have them flash past before I could dismount and ready my camera. Two large, black dogs were running beside the wagon, and the men were waving their sombreros. The third time, I got far enough ahead to get two great shots as they topped a hill and crossed it. They pulled up and hollered in Spanish, "Do we need to slow down?" and "Did I want them to take a picture of me or have a ride?"

I declined their offers and we talked for several minutes. I wanted to ride with them, but they warned me their dogs weren't as hospitable as they were. (Few canines receive rabies vaccinations in Mexico, and certainly not desert ranch dogs.) It was a good break. As I donned my helmet and watched them disappear among the cactus and scrub, I wondered what a typical day was like for them.

I was surprised to discover the road between Juárez and Chihuahua was no longer endless desert. Little towns had sprung up along the way, providing the traveler a variety of independent hotels, restaurants and stores. I took a break at eighty miles and was satisfied I could still take Mexico by bike. My only real problem was the wind. I'd felt like a fishing cork bobbing out of control on some windswept pond during the first miles.

I discovered I could buy Gatorade and bottled water, and was grateful Mexico had become modern enough its small towns now had such amenities. The

25. A road in the desert of Northern Mexico.

Gatorade was refreshing and replenished some of the fluids the desert had sapped from my body. After cooling down, it was time to gas up and check my oil.

At about a hundred miles, I reached the first of many toll roads. Riding alone in the desert, remembering my first stop at a Mexican village, made me wonder what this encounter would be like. Knowing more Spanish now, I had more confidence.

On my first trip, I passed a landscape of rocks and sand and rode far into the night without eating. Not understanding Spanish, I was afraid to order a meal. Finally, I stopped at a Mexican trucker's restaurant, a colorful cement building in the high desert, knowing I had to blindly select something to eat. I still hadn't realized how friendly the people were. As I entered the spartan, poorly lit room, the diners' stares were disconcerting.

The young waitress greeted me with a tentative yet welcoming smile. Embarrassed I understood nothing; I nervously took out my Spanish-English dictionary and tried to order eggs. She stared at me, her formerly sparkling eyes now straining as if to help her understand my words. I glanced around the room. I was obviously alien to their eyes and everyone watched. She became frustrated at my inability to speak her language, but took my order into the kitchen.

I watched and heard her through the tattered curtain serving as a door, as she excitedly told the cook something. In a few moments, she returned with my order. I stared in disbelief at the raw egg and exotic, crimson flower floating in a large goblet. I have no doubt, due to my inadequate pronunciation that was exactly what I'd ordered. The poor village girl was probably terrified and trying to please me. I took the girl and goblet to the kitchen and abandoned any attempt at speaking Spanish. I pointed at the egg in the goblet, then at the stove, and made a rotating motion with my hand. In a few minutes, I had scrambled eggs with *pan* (bread) and *frijoles* (beans), my first meal in Mexico!

5. Chihuahua

About twenty miles before Chihuahua, there's the old
free road. If it's still possible to get on the old route,
if your vehicle isn't overloaded or in danger of overheating, and you don't mind slowing down because of
bumps, potholes and curves, take the free road. Make
sure it's daylight and other traffic is using the road.
It's definitely a section where the highway workers
paved around the potholes. It's exactly like the best
Mexican roads used to look, but it's also more scenic
in an area that provides little but barrenness. In just
a few miles of twists and turns, the old highway runs
back into the toll road, and you ride smooth and free.
My only excitement returning to the good road was a
ten-ton truck on fire. Truck after truck stopped and,
from each, one or two men leaped out with fire extin-
guishers. I started to help, but they looked like they
had enough men and equipment to extinguish it before it spread from the rear tires. It was comforting to
see this aspect of Mexico hadn't changed. Passersby
would still stop and aid a fellow motorist.

Entering Chihuahua with its broad avenues and
traffic, I felt comfortable driving. Police "pull" people
in Chihuahua as they do in the States, causing traffic flow and patterns that resemble American cities.
Even in the easier traffic, I realized the advantage a
car provided in a Mexican city after dark. Motorcycling in the city was intense. There was no way to look

at anything except the traffic. In the open country, the motorcycle is superior —you don't worry about going into a little village or exploring a side road.

I spotted the Motel Nieves (Tecnológico and Ahue-huete), where I'd stayed years ago. It provided good parking and security, although at half the price of a comparable American motel it was no bargain. The location is convenient to the Quinta Luz (a museum featuring the personal effects of Pancho Villa), the Cathedral, the city hall (once called Casa del Cabildo) that has one of the world's largest tables, the regional state museum (known for its archaeological display from Casas Grandes), and the bustling downtown.

At the end of the day, I'd ridden 236 miles entirely through desert. Only the wind was a problem, but I felt I was still tough enough to make it —a good question to answer about oneself. The first day was invigorating, my only discomforts being occasional cramping in my right calf and a sore bottom. During the first leg of a long ride, your rear-end finds a minimum of 239 positions on the bike seat. I'd also gotten too much sun. The redness on my arms told the story, but I hadn't realized the burn was occurring.

I drained glass after glass of lemonade at Rosalinda Zubiate, the hotel restaurant. The sun had dried me out during my ride, and my plastic canteen had proven useless. Eating and drinking at less expensive restaurants increased the risk of dysentery, but extreme thirst made me disregard any precautions. The headwaiter was a short, talkative fellow, Humberto. Typical of many working-class Mexicans, he was proud of his city and glad to meet a foreigner. Humberto didn't mind the rustiness of my Spanish and rambled on in a one-sided conversation.

It wasn't long before I knew all about recent changes in hotel management, the comparative worth

26. It's always exciting to discover what's waiting around the next bend in the road.

of his old and new supervisor, and the most delicious gossip concerning the staff, including a waitress in a red dress upon whom he had designs. Despite the great admiration Humberto had for the shapely lady, she liked the bartender. If I'd had two days, I would've persuaded the guy to act as my guide.

Chihuahua offers the visitor several parking areas to enjoy panoramic views. For many years, the Hotel Victoria was the meeting point for people taking the Copper Canyon train ride. It's a thrilling trip that crosses the land of the Tarahumara Indians and skirts the impressive Copper Canyon from the cold foothills of the Sierras to subtropical terrain. The Victoria still retained its charm in 1993, but now competes with newer hotels.

Waking fresh and well-rested, I realized an element of homesickness for the humdrum rhythm of normal life tugged at me. The isolation of being in another culture and traveling solo allows time for more reflection and increases the sensitivities. I had to put aside thoughts of my family that urged me to return or travel too quickly. I'd have to phone home more than I planned and that would be expensive.

After a filling breakfast, I said good-bye to the people I'd met at the hotel. By noon, the slow travel and loneliness of the road was beginning to bother me. I realized the price paid for being alone at towns or tourist sites. I stopped too often for refreshment, company and respite from the sun. I discovered the price of a Coke in Mexican stores was around 40 cents, but at places for tourists, it could be as much as a dollar.

I thought the Nighthawk was going to flip over twice during the morning. I cut my speed to increase stability. It was dangerous even riding at 45 mph over some of the areas. I worried I'd have to cross the big mountains at 30 to 35 mph.

I stopped at Milas, a quaint hotel/restaurant outside the small town of Cárdenas for a lunch of quesadillas and an RC cola. Several parrots shared the porch with me while I ate and enjoyed the cool shade. I hated restricting my meal to quesadillas while other diners enjoyed delicious-looking plates, but I had to be careful. Mexican dishes vary from state to state and often from town to town. Quesadillas are a simple meal of cheese melted in a tortilla, served pretty much the same throughout Mexico. I find them an excellent choice when I'm not sure purified water is used in food preparation and I need something filling. The Hotel Milas had bargain room rates. I hoped I could find similar accommodations when I stopped for the night.

When I paid, I discovered it was common to have American money —including coins— mixed with change. It complicated determining exactly how much was being spent. Apparently, in northern Mexico, the mixing of American and Mexican money is a result of increased tourism.

South of the town of Delicias, the tourist should take the free road (*"libre"*) to Ciudad Camargo to experience a different and vibrant Mexico. The rivers have been utilized to irrigate the fields via aqueducts and canals. The entire area is abundant with verdant fields and orchards. I rode slow, perhaps 30 or 40 mph. The late morning was hot and I enjoyed the smells of fresh-cut alfalfa while watching men load trucks. The traffic was negligible and I spotted a few elderly *señoras* and eight to ten kids standing on the right past the little bridge ahead. I didn't pay them any attention as I bumped onto the bridge but when bumping back onto the highway the world went black. Thump-thump-thump hit me, frigid water covered me. Momentarily blinded I swerved left but recovered before crossing the center line. I stopped in the road and almost went after some of the kids. The anger quickly subsided and I joined them in laughing at the dunking they'd given me when throwing their buckets of water. I soon discovered these water attacks were a constant at every bridge and the only obstacle I encountered. Little kids hid with pails of water ready to splash every passing motorist. It's okay in a car, but they take a special delight in drenching a motorcyclist. It's unnerving to suddenly be blinded by two or three gallons of water with splash after splash, yet it provides temporary relief from the heat. I made sure my face shield was down when I crossed subsequent bridges.

* * * * * *

The motorcyclist should make a choice at Ciudad Jiménez. The town of Parral, on Highway 45, is about an hour's drive from the more direct route south. It's a wonderfully hilly, crowded small town and the home of Pancho Villa —some even believe Villa's treasure remains hidden in the mountains near the city. Parral does not see nearly the number of tourists who travel more directly south, but it is a warm and interesting town that can quickly captivate a visitor with a spare day or two.

I have not motorcycled this area, but have driven it many times. If one takes Highway 45 to Parral, it's possible to continue on to Durango. The route more or less parallels Highway 49, but is at a higher elevation. Although more scenic, it's also more primitive and offers few amenities for the traveler. Durango is well worth a visit, both for historical reasons and to visit its movie sets.

This alternative route leads to the road I most want to motorcycle in Mexico. Highway 40 runs from Durango to the coastal road near Mazatlan. The distance in a straight line is about 150 miles, but straight it ain't. I rode this highway in 1978 in a Volkswagen van. It took twelve grueling hours and I rarely got out of second gear or reached 25 mph. The highway is probably 7,000 to 8,000 feet above sea level. I don't recall ever hitting a quarter mile length of straightaway. Despite cold, crisp temperatures the drive was so intense my palms were continually wet from nervous sweat. Not a single car, truck or bus overtook me during the entire time. Only three cars passed me going the other way. The scenery was spectacular, yet the narrow twisting road without guard rails made it almost impossible to admire without parking. This highway has been upgraded since I last drove it, but I understand it's still an outstanding and challenging ride for a motorcyclist. The bad news for motorcyclists is a new much better toll road opened in 2013 and there are rumors the old highway may be closed.

Section III

South to Oaxaca

27. A secondary road in the desert.

6. The Ride to Zacatecas

I took the toll road to Jiménez after Camargo. There's nothing of interest on that barren stretch. The wind gave me plenty of problems. An earlier rain made the ride cool and enjoyable, until the sky darkened and lightning cracked in the distance. Riding into the lightning storm, an uneasy, scary feeling gripped me. There wasn't a telephone pole, tree, mesquite bush or even a cactus approaching half my height in sight. I realized a rider on a motorcycle was the tallest thing around. I felt like there was a bull's eye painted on my back.

I reached cover at the toll station before the rain began and spent a few minutes talking with the guards. They said it was six miles to the nearest restaurant. After ten minutes the lightening let up. I decided to make a dash for the restaurant before the rain hit. Big mistake!

Two miles from the tollbooth, a torrent of wind-driven rain lashed across the scrubland. It was a miserable ride, with both rain and wind affecting the bike. Finally, a clean, white restaurant came into sight. Two twenty-year-old boys tended the establishment. They gave me a towel to dry off with, then filled my time with questions. I sipped coffee and answered their inquires while waiting for the storm to pass. My table provided a view of an orchard across the highway. With the pleasant company, I forgot about the rain and stayed until the wind quit bending the trees.

An hour later, the heaviest winds let up, and I took my chances in the light rain. I faced gusts and occasionally the wind picked up for five or ten minutes. New problems arose from the bike's instability, combined with the shoulderless roads. Rear view mirrors are almost as important as seeing ahead on Mexican highways. I watched intently for traffic behind me. If oncoming traffic approached, I could look for places to ease off the road until it passed. When single trucks roared by, I held my position on the road and braced myself to control the bike. Once, as one truck passed me and another simultaneously roared by from the opposite direction, the wind shear hit like a wall, pushing the bike to the right. I fought hard to keep the wheels on the edge of the pavement but bumped along on a rocky bit of shoulder for thirty yards. I fought to keep the bike upright and luckily regained the highway.

I took a break to steady my nerves and tied the backpack differently. The adjustment gave me a little more room to shift around on the seat. I cussed the small side bags again. I should have ditched them before leaving. Back on the road I was much more comfortable with the repositioned pack.

The wind made riding extremely dangerous and I didn't make the distance planned. I stopped after 276 miles at the town of Bermejillo, a two-mile-long strip on the road, twenty miles north of the cities of Gomez Palacio and Torreón. The Hotel Bermejillo is inexpensive with clean rooms, but some people may find it fairly primitive. Still, it beats the alternative of traveling late at night.

Bermejillo's drab main street goes through a metamorphosis and comes alive after dark. Almost every building is a restaurant or shop. Buses and trucks of all sizes and descriptions line the street as the drivers and passengers stop for a meal before continuing their journeys through the lonely desert lands. Young men and women promenade up and down, striking up conversations with passengers. Old women and men sell tamales and tacos from large baskets, while middle-aged ladies ferry supplies balanced on their heads from restaurant to restaurant. Occasionally, a lady of the night will step from one of the darker establishments under some pretense and quickly scamper back inside. Often such "bait" lures a customer from the street. The chatter of hundreds of milling people, mixed with the roar of straining and thunderous diesel engines, is an aspect of Mexican life few visitors experience. The acrid smell of fumes from so many trucks and buses is considered normal by the townspeople. Everyone in Bermejillo works late into the night supplying the needs of the travelers. However, when the morning sun rises, the color and gaiety disappear and the town returns to a dusty strip of colorless buildings.

Not to be left out, I joined the strollers to take in the town. I grabbed a table on the porch of a low-roofed restaurant. Gaily colored lanterns bobbing in the breeze made the place inviting. I ate quesadillas and drank Gatorade served by a buxom forty-year-old waitress. She was wrapped tightly in a vivid yellow skirt and native blouse swirling with a mixture of yellow, red and black. Her attention to detail and passing jabber with bus drivers and truckers would have made her a hit in any restaurant.

Glancing in a few shops along the street, I found prices were considerably lower in a town like Bermejillo. Items from fossils and jewelry to more tourist-type products were cheaper by twenty percent or more than in more prominent towns. Good prices, however, were the least of my concerns. I had about four hundred miles until I reached the coolness of Zacatecas. I'd planned on being there sooner, but the delayed border crossing and the bike's performance in the wind had slowed the journey.

After finishing my meal and again considering my bike problems, I attended to my last duty before sleeping. I rolled up my sleeves and washed my clothes by hand. In the middle of this annoying chore, I decided I'd packed more than was necessary.

I was on the road by 7 a.m., but only made eighty-five miles in the first three hours. The wind remained frustrating. The elevation increased rapidly, causing a marked difference in the weather. I froze all morning. An unpleasant side effect of Mexican travel became evident between Bermejillo and Gómez Palacio. The smell of dead mules, donkeys and cows —the result of unfenced grazing lands— was overwhelming at times. You're safe if you spot loose livestock far ahead and slow down, or stop to watch a man or boy herd his stock across the road. Often, no one is herding the animals and one can bolt into the road at any instant.

Gómez Palacio is an easy town to explore. A modern-style hotel is located on the main street entering town. From there, it's an easy walk to the park and the market. For a newcomer to Mexico, the Gómez Palacio market is an excellent setting to become accustomed to this aspect of Mexican culture. Their market is not as alien to our culture as are many others. The vendors are unhurried and glad to take the time to explain anything from how the tortilla machine works, to how often a parrot lays eggs.

I accidently took the toll road (*autopista*) outside Gómez Palacio and Torreón. The free road was poorly marked and difficult to find. The toll was ridiculously high and I saw absolutely nothing. The road itself is excellent, but there are few cars and no trucks because of the expense. Once on, it was extremely difficult to get off, as they want to collect as much as possible through subsequent tollbooths. I finally exited the *autopista* by cutting across lanes and riding the wrong way on a ramp. Only a motorcycle could have managed the feat safely.

Back on the free road, I stopped at a cafeteria for toast and jelly. It was my fifth stop of the morning simply to get warm. Lifting a piece of toast to my mouth sent a jolt of pain through my arm. With a glance, I saw how badly my arms had burned during the desert ride. They were raw, tender and glowing a feverish red. I pulled a pair of socks from my pack and cut the bottoms off so I could wear them over my arms. They'd offer protection from the sun and provide additional warmth on the morning ride.

Enjoying my toast and jelly, I debated whether to wait for the weather to clear or keep riding in the intermittent drizzle that had been plaguing me. I decided to continue and stop for warmth when I reached another settlement. After a few miles, I started crossing a landscape of large, dome-like foothills. Heavy clouds formed overhead, so close I felt like they were just out of reach. They were different than most clouds I'd ever seen —not gray but more like a mass of dirty-looking cotton someone had pushed together and thrown soot on. Without warning they opened. In seconds I was drenched. Nothing lay ahead but a narrow ribbon of road breaking the barren land.

I continued as rapidly as possible against the driving sheets of water, searching the empty valleys for shelter. A river of water ran down my body until it overflowed my left boot. After several miles in the torrent, I topped a hill where an 18-wheeler had pulled off. I stopped, planning to get under his flatbed, but the trucker waved me into his cab. Handing me a blanket he said, "I am called Luis." We talked for about thirty minutes until the downpour slackened. I left before I was completely warm.

Once I began riding again, my shivering shook the bike so vigorously it made steering difficult. I stopped periodically to walk around and discovered I'd warm up even in the light rain. It was amazing how the high plains air lost its ability to chill when I was off the bike, but each stop still proved frustrating. I could see patches of sunshine warming the earth miles ahead. Each time I remounted, I tried to reach that sunshine. It was like chasing a mirage. I caught a sunlit patch only once, and I warmed rapidly. By sheer will power, I hung on and reached the Motel Ojo de Agua seventy-five miles before Fresnillo.

The motel is a gigantic, futuristic-looking construction. Sloping, white concrete provides an overhead for cars entering. It reminded me of an early fifties movie set with a landing area and hangars for spacecraft. (Carr. 49 Km., 125 Tramo, Fresnillo-Torreón, Juan Aldama, Zac.) I ended up staying by accident. After eating burritos in their expansive restaurant, I learned the motel had long-distance phone service. Despite recent improvements in communications, in 1993, it could still be difficult to find phone or mail service in parts of Mexico. I decided to take advantage of the opportunity to call home.

In Mexico, I quit following the news and worrying about time. I like to forget our world and enjoy the freedom from my normal habits. However, forgetting the world of the clock can be confusing. I realized I both gained and lost a day. I thought it was Friday, June 25th, but discovered it was Thursday June 26th. I guess I broke even. After my call, I discovered the charge for a long distance call was seven dollars, but it was free for guests. My next question was, "How much is a room?"

The *señorita* smiled, "Twenty-one dollars." Despite it being five hours too early to stop, I took a room. Since I was still cold and wet, it wasn't a difficult decision. The rooms were clean and simple, and the restaurant so large it dwarfed the guests even when full. The restaurant has a small bar next to it and the evening regulars keep American visitors well entertained with drinks and friendly conversation.

If you stop at Motel Ojo de Agua, consider visiting two nearby towns. A hundred yards before the motel is a crossroads. A left turn leads to the town of Juan Aldama (a Pemex gas station is on the left). A ride into and around Juan Aldama provides a view seldom seen by tourists. The road winds around the town square with a variety of shops and restaurants lining the far side of the street. The bustling life in such a small town is amazing. People are everywhere. Farmers park and unload fresh produce, bicycles roll about and an occasional mounted rider clops along. It seems a crowd as dense as on Wall Street has come to town. The road is well-marked and circles past cool streams, lush vegetation and fields edging the village before looping back to the main highway. It's enjoyable to stop at the square and walk around, although a visitor will be the object of attention since the little town receives few Americans.

A right turn at the crossroads leads to the town of Miguel Auza. Although the town is small, it's easy to become disoriented. The strange cone-like building on the edge of town is where corn is milled. No sooner than it takes to think about the alien-looking mill than a maze of colorful adobe and cement homes surround you. Narrow rock-paved streets weave and circle in an indecipherable pattern, broken only by odd concrete bridges. It doesn't matter if you get lost. The little lanes will eventually eject you from Miguel Auza. Both towns are worth a slow tour. The shopkeepers are friendly and helpful.

While in the hotel, I watched the flow of life around the crossroad. Local people and people in transit, some in suits, milled about with vaqueros and barefoot farm workers. Elderly ladies with stuffed straw shopping bags gathered on the four corners of the crossroad to catch local and long-distance buses and trucks. They pointedly ignored younger, shapely lasses waiting for northbound buses.

Trucks and buses empty as many as they carry away, and the new people waiting mix with those already at the corner. Some can afford the expensive, long-distance buses. Others wait for the dilapidated fifth and sixth class ancient school buses that will carry them as well as their goats and chickens. A small, white bus runs a regular route between the two towns, and an elderly cab driver in a straw hat stands by to carry three or four customers an hour. He is gone about ten minutes on each fare. It's a routine that's probably gone on since the first stage lines in the 1500s or 1600s. I wonder if the cabbie's ancestors owned the spot and ferried visiting ladies by buggy when they disembarked from a stagecoach.

Returning from a motorcycle ride around Miguel Auza, an odd incident occurred that's becoming more common. A beat-up green station wagon with Cobb County, Georgia plates idled in front of the hotel. It has long been the custom for Americans in rural Mexico to introduce themselves and watch out for fellow Americans. I walked over to see if the people were all right and discovered a car full of Mexicans who had been migrant workers in North Georgia. The parents and grandparents spoke only Spanish, but all the children were equally fluent in English or Spanish.

* * * * *

The morning of June 27th was cold and overcast. My day started miserably. There was no hot water. I dressed and enjoyed *café de olla* in the restaurant. It was the first time I'd found this popular cinnamon-spiked coffee —if unknown to American taste buds— served this far north. I normally drink coffee black but with *café de olla*, I add the customary lump of brown sugar. I told the manager about the water problem. She assured me they would have it corrected within ten minutes. Surprisingly, it was, and I enjoyed a hot shower before getting back on the road. I wanted to make Zacatecas, but was worried about the low, thick cloud cover and wind. The few small trees around the hotel were bending as if they were singers taking bows after a final song. The ride was chilly and occasional showers made it frigid. The stony landscape would have been enjoyable scenery in better weather.

Outside the town of Félix U. Gómez —that's right, it would be like us naming a town Félix U. Unger— is an excellent new hotel called Los Sauces. Their rooms are modern and reasonable. The location is less than an hour from Zacatecas. The complex has a first class restaurant and bar, and provides a truly relaxing atmosphere. The waitress was a petite, Mexican beauty who insisted I should sightsee locally before going on. She and the owner were full of questions about touring on a motorcycle. Had I been in an automobile, I would have stayed and commuted back and forth to the sites of Zacatecas just to enjoy the peacefulness, cleanliness and charm of the area.

I hated leaving their company but was soon on

my way. There is nothing like the exhilaration of being on a motorcycle on a narrow, two-lane Mexican highway, with one car passing you traveling 80 mph while another car passes him going a 100 mph. Obviously the cyclist gives ground and skirts the shoulder. The motorcyclist must adjust to cars not pulling into the other lane, but passing within a yard as they whiz by. Your eyes must stay glued to your rearview mirrors; you cannot take it for granted you will be the only person in your lane. Still, it's better than years ago when Mexican drivers passed within inches of a motorcycle.

It was a bone-chilling ride with rain threatening continuously. I needed my leather jacket, including its winter lining. Because of the cold and the barmaid's encouragement, I stopped in a downtown park in Fresnillo to walk around and regain some of my body heat. It took two hours for the weather to clear. During that time the park filled with activity. Men and boys lounged on the benches, and hordes of young schoolgirls and women strolled through on various errands. Half the people in the park wanted to talk about the United States and the motorcycle. I spent most of my time talking with a young man named Guillermo, and a sixty-year-old engineer. He was an out-of-work mining engineer and explained it was hard times, as most of the mines were shut down. Both men voiced the same economic worries as we Americans do. They were concerned metal prices had fallen so low that Mexican companies were buying foreign steel.

Fresnillo is a typical Mexican town that has had little influence from American visitors. The people are open and friendly. They have a busy market and three main *jardines,* or shaded town squares. *Jardines* are used for simply resting, meeting friends, watching the beauty of life, letting small children play and providing a place for young lovers to meet. At night, many *jardines* host music groups for the loungers to enjoy. As with most places in Mexico, the friendliness came across immediately. My two new friends offered to give me a tour of their city and put me up for the night. The offer was tempting, and having a native act as a guide always opens more doors than any lone tourist can find. Unfortunately, I had to decline their offers to take advantage of a break in the weather.

28. The city of Zacatecas. Note the level of the car passing above to gauge the steepness of the city.

7. Zacatecas

Zacatecas, 8,200 feet above sea level, loomed ahead as darkness fell. A cold wind knifed through me, bouncing and bobbing the bike with a forceful, shearing effect. The majestic colonial city, known for its pink stone facades, silver mining, and historic buildings, did not seem inviting. The last thirty miles were negotiated in light rain at less than 35 mph, with the continuous prospect of being blown off the road. Thankfully, the four lane highway was safer than most. I'd hoped the cuts through the mountaintops would reduce the effect of the wind, but the slits made it worse as the shifting wind began hitting from various angles.

In Zacatecas the main road was scary in the dark, with three to four lanes zipping each way up and down the hills of the city. I began pulling off and following each mass of traffic until the next group came up behind me. Then I would look for another safe area to pull off. I was prepared for the hills and curves of Zacatecas in dry weather. Instead, shimmering light weakly reflected off the slick, wet roads. With the Mexican method of driving wide open and slamming on brakes at the last second, a stranger on a bike at night feels at an awesome disadvantage.

After a few wrong turns, I located the Hotel Colón on López Velarde 508 and López Mateos 105. It's a small building, between two streets, and immacu-

29. One of Zacatecas' wider streets.

lately kept. The deskman ignored my wetness and filthy jeans —black below the knees from oil and tar kicked up from the highway— and showed me where to park and chain my bike. Dropping my gear on the tile floor of my room, my eyes caught the heavy woolen blanket, and I knew I was all right. I would get warm and wash my clothes before leaving. At about twenty dollars, the room was a bargain.

The Hotel Colón is about half a block from a more expensive and elegant hotel once called the Gallery (Blvd. López Mateos). After a hot shower revitalized me, I walked to the Gallery to eat at their elegant restaurant, which features a fantastically huge chandelier. The food and service were first class, but unfortunately the price of the meal was almost as much as a room at the Colón.

Later, I walked up the street and found the bar Conquistador. It was difficult to miss. Music poured out the open door and mixed with the sounds of pedestrians and nighttime city traffic. It was a typical Mexican nightclub, and a talented singer with a guitar entertained two people with dates as well as fifteen other men spread about the tables drinking. When the staff realized I was American, Mexican hospitality prevailed. The waiters and barmaids were extra attentive.

It is virtually impossible to tell someone how to get around in Zacatecas. The city has enough twists and turns to make a slinky envious. Having been lost on many of Zacatecas' zigs and zags, I've learned different maps of the city often agree on only major points, and the streets listed don't always correspond. But if there's an agreeable city to be lost in, it's Zacatecas.

A free map is available from the tourist office across the street from the cathedral. Young college students, somewhat fluent in English, work in the office. Parking can be troublesome if you tour Zacatecas by automobile, but a motorcycle solves that problem.

Zacatecas is a flagstone-paved city that lacks any modern constructions or franchises in its central area to mar its colonial beauty. Many of the hotels offer local tours, but it's not necessary if you have a little time to explore. Most of the sites are conducive to a walking tour. On Hidalgo Avenue is the Basilica Cathedral. Considered the best baroque architecture built in Mexico during the 1700s, its facade is covered with carvings. Facing the side of the Cathedral are the Plaza de Armas and the Government Palace, first-rate examples of civil colonial architecture. To the left are the Calderón Theater, Goitia Square and the mall, El Mercado. Among a host of items for sale in this unusual upstairs mall are precious stones, leather goods, candy and local wines. There are also many souvenir shops on the street level.

Outside El Mercado is the Acropolis Café. This little restaurant is a dandy place to rest and eat when walking the city. It has excellent coffee —once widely considered the best in Mexico— and tasty pastry. Years ago, coffee in Mexico was about half milk, very sweet and served lukewarm. Frequent visitors knew

30. Near the Zacatecas market on a slow morning.

American-style coffee was available at the Acropolis.

The service is excellent and reminds one of an old-fashioned American diner or café. The waitresses are like American working girls featured in 1930s movies. The entire place is a constant beehive of activity.

Across the *mercado* or market from the Acropolis, is a second floor balcony restaurant. It's an inviting spot to relax over a snack and join the locals. They utilize the long open restaurant to see and be seen by people promenading along the street forty-five feet below.

A leisurely, twenty-minute walk from the Cathedral and past the Plaza de Armas is the Founders' Fountain. Hidalgo Street merges and becomes Juan de Tolosa. (Remember to take a left when walking back to avoid getting lost. Vehicles have to go straight when returning. Drivers must look for a one-way street to carry them left and back to the center.) Zacatecas is an old city, and the streets can easily confuse tourists. Expect to lose your way. Beyond the Founders' Fountain is Saint Frances, once a temple and monastery that now holds the Rafael Coronel Museum.

My first day in Zacatecas was wonderfully confusing. Delight after delight was the reward for my

31. A statue honoring the Mexican Revolution of 1910 at La Bufa, Zacatecas.

exploring. The city is cut by narrow pedestrian lanes that were once roads for men on horseback. A wrong turn makes no difference. The entire city is worth seeing, and each wrong turn reveals pleasant surprises. After spending the evening watching street-side entertainers, I slept soundly, hoping for a second day as rewarding as the first.

Waking early, I wanted to see the remainder of Zacatecas. I'd stopped in the city several times, but this was my first opportunity to really study this jewel unknown to most Americans. Santo Domingo Square must be visited and can be reached by taking Veyna Alley from the *mercado* and cathedral area. Important buildings ring this square, including the Santo Domingo Temple, which houses historic paintings in gold leaf.

Next to the temple is one of the most important museums in Latin America —the Pedro Coronel Mu-

32. Church at La Bufa, Zacatecas.

seum. Once inside, don't let the lack of signs or the initial sparseness distract you. It takes several hours to view what's waiting. Wander through the libraries of ancient tomes and the diminutive inside garden, but continue on. Picasso, Rouault and the works of many other artists await you. There is an excellent exhibit of pre-Columbian art and statues, a room demonstrating a variety of the masks used in festivals throughout Mexico, and a number of wonderful bullfighting drawings by Franciso de Goya y Lucientes. "Exceptional" doesn't do justice to the work.

Among a host of early colonial artifacts was an ornate and mysterious-looking lady's box. It was a puzzle. I counted seventeen openings and could only wonder where the secret door might be. The museum also has outstanding exhibits of ancient art, covering pretty much the entire spectrum of the ancient world from Egypt, Rome and Mesopotamia to Thailand and India. The African exhibit definitely is not influenced by the politically correct mentality now in vogue in

33. Aqueduct that once quenched the thirst of Spanish colonists in Zacatecas.

America. It was the most accurate and fascinating African exhibit I'd ever seen and surpasses anything I've heard of in the United States. The spears, masks, bows and arrows exuded the raw power African natives needed to survive without modern weapons.

On Sunday, I was up at 7:30 a.m., hoping to see the remainder of the city. The traffic wasn't bad so, after a walk to gain my bearings, I took the bike. I wanted to go to the chapel overlooking the city at a site called La Bufa. The sky was cloud-covered. I ate breakfast at Las Pampas, a steak and seafood restaurant off the main drive. It was a fancy place, especially for this part of Mexico in 1993, and is more a nighttime bar/restaurant than a breakfast place. Prices ranged from a shrimp cocktail for about five bucks to a rib eye, T-bone (spelled T-Bonne) or *carne a la tampiquena* (a typical Mexican steak dish) at close to American prices.

The ride to La Bufa is a motorcyclist's delight with its ever-changing vistas and curves. As you zoom up, be aware of the possibility of hitting lose gravel in some of the turns. Before 8 a.m., there are few visitors. The plazas and parking area begin filling after 10 a.m. If going before midday, bring a coat

34. The Hotel Quinta Real in is built around the original 1866 San Pedro bullring.

or heavy sweater and plan to stay two or three hours. Walking around the bluff provides an ever-altering panoramic view as the city below becomes a colorful quilt that changes with the sun and clouds.

Until recently, motorcycles were almost exclusively used within or near cities. Mexican after Mexican expressed surprise I was traveling by bike. Occasionally, I would hear a North American had passed a few months before on a motorcycle, but I hadn't seen any other riders. At La Bufa, a guy pulled up on a new 250 Nighthawk. Judging by his packs, he was obviously touring. I discovered he was a Mexican trying out his new bike by making a round trip from San Luis Potosí. He too, had problems with his bike's performance in the wind.

The church of the Virgin de los Remedios is on La Bufa and worth a lingering visit. Take the time to enjoy both the manicured courtyard and the paintings and sculpture within the chapel. There are small

35. The majestic lobby of the Hotel Quinta Real in Zacatecas.

shops and restaurants throughout the site, but no one is pushy selling their wares. The vendors offered me a welcome surprise when I asked for information about some aspect of the site. Aiding me was their first priority; selling was a distant second.

The museum at La Bufa contains many articles from the Mexican Revolution. There are some excellent photos from 1913-14, including one of a grisly pile of corpses taken after they faced the firing squad. It's not a vast museum but definitely worth the small entry fee. Don't count on meeting countrymen in the area. On the visitors' register, I noticed only two Americans had entered the museum during the three days before my visit.

Leaving La Bufa, I discovered a secret to learning Zacatecas' layout. There is much less traffic in Zacatecas's *centro* on Sunday, especially during siesta. I was able to get about easier than I ever had on previous trips. The lull in traffic allowed a better chance to

36. The Hall of Columns at La Quemada archaeological site. The columns were apparently six to nine feet higher sixty years ago.

learn the layout of the city.

There's no question that visiting Zacatecas is a step back into medieval Europe. Narrow alleys and walkways abound. The side streets rival San Francisco's in steepness. All the streets are flagstones, perhaps a foot and a half square, and all a dirty, faded red.

By the early evening, I was worn out from my trek about the city. Instead of looking for nightlife, I turned in. Up at 8 a.m., I was ready to explore again and found the Quinta Real Hotel quite by accident. I was going to see the aqueduct and adjoining park, when I noticed an entranceway under the aqueduct to what I took to be a country club. I stuck my head in and realized it was a hotel with little in the way of advertising. It was a great accident, and I spent until noon enjoying the Quinta Real Hotel. The staff was helpful and provided ample information. I have an aversion to paying more than twenty or thirty dollars for a hotel room. Despite staying in the Mark

37. Ancient stone walls at La Quemada.

Hopkins in San Francisco and many other expensive inns over the years, I've rarely felt the cost was worth the difference over staying in a budget motel. I say that because, within a few feet of entering the Quinta Real, I knew I was in something really special. The gleaming curved corridor dotted with alcoves and plants was breathtaking. I quickly found the front desk and was quoted a price of almost 200 dollars per night. Having only seen maybe fifty feet of the hotel, I knew the price wasn't exorbitant.

If Zacatecas lacked its other magnificent sites, this hotel alone —once featured in Ripley's "Believe It or Not"— would be worth visiting. The hotel is actually a bullring built in 1866. In 1988, the owners began turning the bullring into a hotel. It appears no cost was spared in making the transition. The hotel opened on February 23, 1989, and is stunning in its elegance. While looking at the many in-house shops, enjoying the luxury, I glanced up and considered the history. A medieval aqueduct crossed part of the bullring. Despite the guests and a staff of 115 men and

38. Temple at the La Quemada archaeological site not far from the city of Zacatecas .

39. A stone wall at La Quemada.

women, the sheer size ensures quiet and provides spots to be entirely alone.

I couldn't afford to stay at the Quinta Real, but I had to see more of this special hotel. After some discussion with the lovely young lady at the desk, I discovered the standard suite could be had for as low as $150 per night. On some future trip, I would stay at least a night. I didn't inquire about the costs of the Master Suites or Presidential suite. The regular rooms were decorated and furnished luxuriously enough to satisfy all my needs, but I continued speaking with the young woman. The main fiesta at Zacatecas occurs on the second and third week of September. Reservations should definitely be made during that period. Never stop talking in Mexico. After I switched subjects, I found out more about the prices. If you are persistent, it's possible to get a cheaper rate on a Sunday, Monday or Tuesday.

I decided to eat breakfast there to see more of the hotel. I walked the rounded corridors and relaxed over a meal in the dining room. It was a step back to a civility and elegance I hadn't realized still existed. White-gloved servers work amid wonderful paintings, colorful crockery and deep green plants that adorn the tri-level dining room of powder-pink walls. A breakfast of eggs, ham, rolls and toast, juice and American style coffee with unlimited refills satisfied me completely. 1930s American dance music and classical Spanish music played quietly in the background. The restaurant has an inside and outside section, so you may look down onto the bullring. While you overlook the arena where matadors once fought fine, fierce *toros,* you cannot help feeling you're back in time, perhaps even sitting in a Roman coliseum.

The name of the hotel's bar, "El Botarel," refers to the type of arch found in the bar. It is definitely unique. El Botarel is located where the bulls were kept before entering the ring. The chairs and tables throughout the bar were comfortable and in sections that provided a sense of intimacy to the guests. Throughout the bar, I always relaxed and enjoyed myself, despite having the sensation of being in catacombs.

The bar has live entertainment each night. The Quinta Real provides different types of music and has a resident trio. Other musicians entertain at special times including, "*La Tambora,*" or "Big Drum," which is a special music common to Northern Mexico.

I've barely touched on the sites in Zacatecas. Nearly every building is historic. Among several silver mines is the El Eden mine. It is open for visitors and rails them in behind a mining locomotive four days a week. El Eden also features an underground disco in a cavern deep inside the mountain. A Swiss cable car crosses the city at a height of 179 feet. Many other museums and smaller historical sites are within easy driving distance, including the famous Indian ruin of La Quemada, (called Chicomostoc on some maps), less than an hour's drive from the city.

The archaeological zone of La Quemada is just off Highway 70. The ruins stand in gigantic proportions and offer a challenge to the visitor. See if you can spot the ruins from the road before seeing the entry sign. The main site consists of several masonry platforms built on a large hill in the middle of an arid valley. They blend in with the terrain so well that only the sharpest-eyed person will spot them from more than a quarter mile. There is a network of over 102 miles of ancient roadways leading to lesser sites. Archeologists have established the time period for La Quemada as ranging from 300 to 1200 A.D.

Because of its remoteness, there are many theories concerning La Quemada's history. Those are easily looked up but I prefer the story an Indian farmer related. The gentleman said his grandfather claimed seven tribes lived in and farmed the valley. When more warlike and savage peoples raided the valley, the tribes would retreat to the safety of their hill-fortress. A defensive rampart twelve feet thick and twelve feet high was built on the north slope. The defensive nature of much of the site combined with the structures blending in to appear a natural part of the hill indicate the old Indian's history may be more accurate than some of the professionals' theories.

Some of La Quemada's most noted features include the following:

• The Hall of Columns: An enclosure measuring

135 by 107 feet. The purpose of the area is unknown although some speculate it was used for ceremonial human sacrifice.

- The Main Causeway: Sprawls 1,300 feet from the Plaza near the Hall of Columns.
- The Ball Court: A typical Meso-American structure 233 feet long and 50 wide. The side walls are nearly nine feet thick.
- The Offering Pyramid: A steep structure 33 feet high.
- The Stairway: Living quarters, platforms and walls.

Zacatecas to Guadalajara

There are two main routes. The most direct route is Highway 54. This is not the route I took, but I believe it is the best purely for motorcycling. Highway 54 does not go through any large cities. It is more mountainous and the scenery is spectacular.

The route I picked was Highway 45 to Highway 80. It goes through more large towns and does not include the serpentine roads that drop several thousand feet to valley floors before winding their way back up.

40. The Cathedral on the Plaza de la Patria in Aguascalientes.

Mexico by Motorcyle: An Adventure Story and Guide

8. Aguascalientes and Tepatitlán

It was an easy drive to Aguascalientes through rich farm, cattle and dairy country. Highway 54 is one of the best free roads in Mexico. In the state of Aguascalientes, it even has wide shoulders. On the left, entering Aguascalientes, is a new modern hotel. It's an easy drive to the center of town and offers all the amenities one could expect. I was tempted to stay but, as it was early, I decided to find lodging in the downtown area.

Once settled in the Hotel Reforma, I walked to the Church of San Antonio. Unfortunately, it was closed until the next morning. The church is a must-see. It was built by an untrained architect who mixed neoclassic, byzantine, baroque and a few unknown styles. The inside is noted for offering a collection of oddities in an effort at decoration.

I regretted arriving too late in the day. There were three other churches I also wanted to see, but I wouldn't accomplish it this trip. Viewing so many churches in a single day would be overwhelming. I spent much of the evening walking around Aguascalientes. Despite having a population of over 800,000, I rarely felt I was in a large city. The main square goes to sleep about 9:30 p.m.

I was ready for a bit of nightlife, and knew I'd have to find friends or be willing to explore on my own. I hadn't seen a single foreign tourist in the city. The few Mexicans I met weren't fluent in English. I was on my own and decided to find the area where the mariachis play. After getting directions, I crossed the square in front of the Cathedral and took the alley beside the Hotel Imperial. It turned into a real street, called 5 de Mayo, running next to the city's three-story mall. I followed the dark, deserted street. The sensation of being back in time filled me as it often does when walking alone between ancient buildings. After seven blocks, I reached a darkened park. Several mariachis groups were playing on the far side and a growing crowd of revelers enjoyed the evening. Pretty girls, young boys and women were weaving between the clusters of people, serving food and drinks. I strolled over and, typical of Mexican hospitality, was quickly welcomed and encouraged to join the festivities.

I slept until 9:15 a.m. the following morning. The banter of a dozen parrots and songbirds made waking a pleasure. The Hotel Reforma and a more expensive one are on Nieto, just off the square, down from the Cathedral and off Galeana. I chose to stay at the Hotel Reforma, the old-style, downtown Mexican hotel. The two-story hotel is built around a tiled central courtyard that houses a forest of plants. Birdcages hang from the upstairs veranda and from large plants during the day. Despite the narrow entryway, a car can squeeze inside if a patron feels unsafe about parking on the street. It might not be for everyone, despite costing less than twenty dollars a night but for me, the lively birds definitely made it the right choice.

The rooms have 25-foot ceilings. Each has its own ancient, but clean and functional bathroom. The interior is always cool and comfortable. An elderly lady and her son, who speaks some English, operate

41. An inside view of one of the many beautiful churches in Aguascalientes.

the Reforma. There is a clerk on duty twenty-four hours a day.

About half a block down Galeana on the left sat a little European-style restaurant called El Zodiaco. A small shrimp cocktail cost about three dollars and an order of pancakes even less. The cleanliness, efficiency and orderliness allowed me to relax my cautions in food selection and enjoy several large meals.

For a slice of Mexican life, take advantage of the fruit stands throughout Aguascalientes. They are small, stall-like places that sell only fruit. Simply step in off the street and point out what you want. The man will wash and then squeeze your selection —carrots, pineapple, oranges, mango— into a large juice glass. Don't risk a fruit drink mixed with water. Say, "*No agua, por favor!*"

While in Aguascalientes, you definitely want to lounge around the central square. A motorcycle can pull onto the broad expanse and park without causing any problem. The ornate, baroque Cathedral dominates the square. Inside is a famous painting of the Last Supper by Miguel Cabrera. I often spend an enjoyable half-hour sitting in the Hotel Francia's restaurant, or in the shaded part of the square, watching the mass of humanity cross the square while the sun plays against the Cathedral.

Next door is the Teatro Morelos, where many of Mexico's revolutionaries, including Pancho Villa, gathered in 1914. The leading revolutionaries could not reach any agreement in their famous convention and Villa offered a novel solution. He suggested he and his main opponent, Carranza, have themselves executed to resolve their differences. Carranza —being a true politician— put the safety of his own carcass before the welfare of his country. He avoided the Teatro Morelos.

My favorite building is the Palacio de Gobierno, or state house. I've visited the building —built forty-five years after the first pilgrims stepped ashore at Plymouth— a half dozen times. Still, I feel like a child making a new discovery with each visit, especially in the early morning. Light rays filter through the two-story, arched and columned building, reflecting against the red and pink stone used in its construction. A huge staircase in the center of the open room allows access to the upper floor. You're free to walk about, unnoticed by the people beginning their days' work. I cannot imagine anyone who would not be struck by the beauty and massiveness of the building.

I shook my head in disbelief. It had quit raining as I entered Aguascalientes. Now a light rain was starting as I left at noon. I had ridden about 100 miles by 4:30 p.m. when the drizzle finally quit. The road meanders through rolling country with few trees, and there is a stretch with green mesas. I was reassured, realizing there would be no problem finding lodging. Many inviting hacienda-style and coun-

42. Biking in Mexican towns and cities is a special challenge.

try-style hotels dotted the route. A number of small towns off the highway also had hotels. It was enjoyable motorcycling country as the earth's contours provided easy curves. I was able to enjoy the scenery more than usual. I easily passed clusters of traffic as heavy trucks backed cars up on the hills and curves. I'd then have several minutes of auto-free road until I leapfrogged the next string of backed-up cars.

More heavy rain hit at the *cuota* (toll station) forty miles before Guadalajara. I pulled off at a modern combination convenience store and coffee shop to warm up. The three ladies working there were talkative and full of questions about motorcycling. The oldest woman, about forty, kept my coffee cup full while I relaxed. They insisted I should stay in the nearby city of Tepatitlán. They were persuasive salesladies, claiming their city was lovely, with the most beautiful girls in all Mexico. They added the Plaza Hotel was the best place to stay. Because of the hour and the rain, I took their friendly advice. Who am I to pass up seeing the most beautiful girls in all Mexico? The ride into Tepatitlán was easy on wide, one-way streets. I checked into the excellent Plaza Hotel (Hidalgo 63 C.P. 47600 Centro). The price made my stay a wise decision. A ten-percent discount is given on request. The rooms are the equivalent of an above-average U.S. hotel room, but are a third larger.

Tepatitlán features one of the cleanest central plaza areas I've seen in Mexico. A colorful government palace and several historic churches front part of the square. Natives boast Father Miguel Hidalgo —the leader of Mexico's Independence War— was from the city and fought from the church off their square.

While filling me in on local history, the hotel receptionist recommended a bar that turned out to be one of the most American-looking bars I've visited in Mexico. It was frequented by an amiable crowd. The two fellows behind the bar, Miguel and Oscar, both spoke some English. We carried on a conversation for four hours in both languages. I met the owner of the hotel and his son, a physician, among a host of other townspeople. Surprisingly, several groups of friendly, young women entered and chatted with the patrons over drinks. In most of Mexico, it's rare to see unescorted women in a bar. However, the practice was well tolerated and the young women always stayed together. The city is close enough to the metropolitan area of Guadalajara that many of the societal restrictions governing female behavior are changing.

When the bar closed about midnight, the bartenders and a half-dozen patrons wanted to show me their local late-night club. We walked a short distance and climbed a stairway to a second floor club with musicians. The bouncer decided to check me for weapons. He acted upset when I pulled a four-inch buck knife from my pocket. I think he was hoping to gain a bribe, but the people with me chided him. They explained I carried it because I had to cross lonely country on a motorcycle. The guy relented, but said he'd have to hold the knife.

The club scene was much more American than Mexican. I didn't want to drink that evening. But as happened at the first bar, person after person wanted to buy me a mixed drink instead of the Coke I sipped. I pointed to my shoulder each time and shouted *inyección* or injection, to be heard over the music. We left about three in the morning. I could tell it broke the guard's heart when I asked for my knife.

Tepatitlán is quiet and picturesque, with a population of between 150,000 and 180,000. Travelers should consider it as a place to stay when visiting Guadalajara because of the lower hotel prices. It is about an hour by free road and a half-hour by toll road. I'm still debating if the city has the most beautiful women.

43. Guadalajara's magnificent Metropolitan Cathedral.

9. Guadalajara

On July first I arrived at Guadalajara, the home of my old friends Habvi and Socorro. Their three sons are wonderful little boys. Mauricio, the youngest, had a black eye and a half. He'd fallen into a 12-foot deep concrete pit chasing a ball. His face hit a piece of wood straddling the pit about a third the way down, flipping and then landing him feet first. He was lucky to only have a black eye and swollen face. His accident was an important reminder for me. While I don't worry about crime in Mexico, there are few laws governing construction sites or property upkeep. I stay alert for dangling electric wires or broken sidewalks when taking a stroll.

Two friends were planning to visit Guadalajara while I was there. I checked on hotels for them. The best I could do was the Hotel Malibu. It's modern in every way, but built in the old Mexican style, with arches and columns. The rooms surround an interior garden, making it appear warm and inviting. Located on Avenida Vallarta, the hotel is next door to La Gran Plaza and convenient to Plaza Galerías, Plaza del Sol and the downtown area.

There are many places to stay in Guadalajara at over $100 per night. The only two I might consider at that price are the El Tapatío and the Quinta Real. I made several trips to El Tapatío and suggest any visitor have at least a few meals there and enjoy the

The Malinche Complex

There are insights into the Mexican subconscious mind Americans should be aware of if they hope to understand Mexico. These capsules of truth run deep in the native mind, soul and character. They define the inner psyche of the population far better than any discussion of Mexican politics or economy. One is the Malinche complex.

There are a number of rival theories that explain the Malinche complex, but this is how it was explained to me.

Malinche was a Maya girl sold to the Aztecs as a slave. When Conquistador Hernán Cortés defeated the Tlaxcalans, Malinche became his slave and interpreter. Cortés conveyed his messages to a Spanish priest who had been shipwrecked off Yucatán years before. The priest translated from Spanish to Maya, and Malinche then spoke in the local indigenous languages. She became Cortés' mistress and bore him the son, who would become the first New World citizen to try to throw off the chains of the European monarchies.

Because Malinche disavowed the old, Indian Mexico for the new, she has given her name to *malinchismo,* the Mexican mind-set that anything from other countries is superior to that produced in Mexico.

It's a ridiculous concept. Mexicans know it's absurd, but it still pervades their being.

If you're lucky enough to have upper middle-class Mexican friends and visit, you'll probably see the Malinche complex in action. You may want to see the wonderful colonial cathedrals or eat at what we think of as a romantic Mexican restaurant but, more likely, your hosts will take you to the newest, most modern, antiseptic edifice available.

Subconsciously, they aren't showing you the old Mexico with its warts, but rather displaying a better Mexico, because it's more modern. You probably won't agree, and if they stop to think about it, they won't either.

44. Enjoying Guadalajara's Plaza Tapatía.

view from the restaurant and lounge. Hotel prices are high in Guadalajara, but a host of less expensive hotels can be located with a bit of searching. Several of the most expensive hotels in 1993 actually have lower prices today, as competition became a reality.

One can find quality rooms in most areas of Mexico for about twenty-five to thirty dollars per night, but not in Guadalajara or Mexico City. Guadalajara is expensive. The price of a meal in better restaurants, considering food portions, is more expensive than in the States. The exception is fruit juices in the restaurants.

When my friends arrived, Habvi insisted we eat at the new Sanborn's located in a modern mall. It wasn't as pleasing as the original Sanborn's. There are now many more of the restaurants in the city, but the Mexican mind-set, or the Malinche complex, means the newer the better. I didn't find the food up to the usual quality, but the others had no complaints. Relaxed at my friends' home, I reassessed what I car-

Notes on Foods

It's ironic. Not today, but there have been times I've found better quality old-time cheeseburgers in Mexico than in the States. This wasn't the case forty years ago. Mexicans had just discovered the notion of the American hamburger, and many restaurants featured signs saying *hamburguesas*. The problem was they had no idea what this special American food was. You might be served a hamburger of fish, ham or anything else. Since then, they've learned. Often their hamburgers are far better than the ultra-processed version in modern America. For a few years, such combinations of chicken or fish *hamburguesas* disappeared from menus but Mexicans enjoyed those versions of hamburgers and they have reappeared in many restaurants.

Preservatives are not as commonly used in Mexico. We really don't realize the tastes, texture, flavors and actual delight we've lost until we bite into their version of our pancakes. But savoring pancakes is hardly the end of the story. Bread and pastries will spoil quickly, but the rich taste makes one question if we've really gained with the use of artificial colors, flavors and preservatives.

The sugar in Mexico is not as refined as our sugar. It's supposed to be better for you than our variety. It provides a slightly different, but satisfactory taste. Most Americans will find the bakery products a bit less sweet, but equally as delicious.

ried and made a bad decision for a lone biker. My plastic poncho was in tatters, but still shielded me from some of the wind. I kept it, but decided to send everything extra back to the States with my friends. I halved my clothes and gave my army backpack to Habvi's oldest son. I felt I had enough left to complete the trip, and the reduction in gear would pro-

45. A reflecting pool in Plaza Tapatía in downtown Guadalajara.

vide more room for comfortable riding.

* * * * *

Guadalajara, founded in 1542, is known as the "Pearl of the West." The population in the metropolitan area is estimated at between 5 and 9 million. Despite the numbers, the city retains a small town charm. The people are friendly to Americans, and there are an abundance of things to do and sites to see.

Surrounded by villages —many favored by Canadian and American retirees—Lake Chapala is thirty miles from Guadalajara. The lake is sixty miles long, a little over twelve miles in width and nestles in the mountains above the city. Numerous fine restaurants and hotels surround it. A day can pass quickly investigating and enjoying the area.

Within the city, the Plaza del Sol area has the first open-air shopping center of its kind in Mexico, built in 1968 and covering several city blocks. The varied shops and many of their wares are unique to

American visitors. It's an excellent location to use as an anchoring point while learning the city. My favorite Sanborn's restaurant is across from the mall. Despite being in a bustling area, it's a luxurious setting for a meal. I always take a veranda table. However, it can be chilly at night. The Iztepete pyramid is just a ten-minute bike ride on Mariano Otero from Plaza del Sol. The site is small by Mexican standards but, if you've never seen the more famous indigenous archaeological monuments, these neglected ruins are worth a visit.

We window-shopped the better part the day in Tlaquepaque, which is an artisan town swallowed by the city. The central street is closed to automobile traffic. The old mansions lining the lane have been turned into showrooms and studios for fine craftsmen. Although many of the products are affordable, you can also find exquisite works —such as gilded hand-carved tables— in excess of seven thousand 1993 dollars. I can only wonder what the cost of such handwork would be at home. At one end of the street turned pedestrian walkway is a huge circular building known as El Parián. Different restaurants operate separate sections and have tables on the inside and outside. The food is pure Mexican. While you rest from shopping over a meal or snack, mariachi groups move from table to table providing entertainment.

The next day, I parked the bike and we took a cab to the heart of the city. The Cathedral, began in 1568, has four notable plazas surrounding it to form a cross. The entire ten blocks linking the Cathedral with the Cabañas Cultural Center is a shopping area called Plaza Tapatía. Right off the plaza is the central Libertad Market in the San Juan de Dios neighborhood, which demands a visit. You can browse the shops on all three levels without vendors pressuring

46. Ever wonder how tequila starts? An agave field in Central Mexico in the 1970s.

you to buy something, as is the case at tawdry border markets.

After a long day of shopping and sightseeing, I decided to take my friends somewhere special and inexpensive, if not exotic, for supper. Two short bike rides brought us to El Pollo Pepe. We entered a small, open building, walking past several chickens roasting over glowing coals on a large, rectangular grill. After selecting soft drinks in flavors not found at home, our meal was quickly served. Using tortillas and fingers, we enjoyed some of the tastiest chicken we'd ever eaten. Their special marinade results in a delicious product. I've never discovered why the roasting doesn't dry out the meat.

10. The Ride to Morelia

On July 4th, I left my U.S. friends in the Tonalá Market with Paulo, the oldest son of my Mexican friends. The Tonalá market is stand after stand, store after store, and block after block of every handcraft and item imaginable. Many of the ceramics in the region are produced in this twenty- by thirty-block area. The pottery remains first-class and the blown glassware and papier-mâché can be purchased for only a fraction of what they cost on the border. Villagers travel in from outlying areas to sell their wares. Packed with buyers and sellers, the market's streets, alleys and lanes feel narrower than they actually are. My friends were delighted with the number of shops they could explore and the continuous bustle of human activity. I had followed their cab on my bike and was pleased to discover how easily I could ride around in the crowded market.

With some regret, I left during the afternoon. I hoped my friends would be all right for the next three days without me to look out for them. In the short time my arms were exposed to the sun that first day back on the road, they became very red where the skin had already peeled. I would have to be exceedingly careful from now on.

An hour out of Guadalajara, the sky darkened and gusting wind, lightning and thunder followed. Fortunately, I spotted the restaurant Casa Blanca sitting off the road. It was open-air with brick arches and tile roofing, a style of restaurant commonly located just out of Mexican cities. They are popular for late afternoon meals and for family meals on Sunday. With the afternoon rush over, only two families were eating. I waited out the storm, talking with the owner's son. It gave me time to reflect on what a wholesome family Habvi and Socorro have. I'd rarely seen Mexicans discipline or even raise their voices to their children, but they sure turn out well.

I had a choice when the rain finally quit and, although it was the wrong road, it wouldn't be a big delay. I detoured and stayed in Tepatitlán again. On the fifth, I got off to a late start and cut across on smaller roads traveling through Arandas, Irapuato and a host of smaller towns and villages to Salamanca. For the first time since I left the desert, there was no rain and the weather was perfect for motorcycling. The smaller, unmarked roads reminded me of my first trip through Mexico. I passed people working in fields and many small trucks loaded with the local harvest. It was obvious few tourists traveled these roads.

At noon, I stopped in a chalet-looking restaurant-bar in the center of a small village. Pulling off the highway, I slowly bumped a hundred yards over cantaloupe sized boulders that paved the parking area. The restaurant was airy and cool inside, but the employees were warm and friendly. After getting directions from the manager, I discovered my back tire was flat. I asked the manager about a place across the street that worked on truck tires. He said, "They're too lazy, but you can try."

A few moments later, I knew the manager was right. He suggested a guy on the edge of the village who worked on motorcycles. As is the case in many small Mexican villages, the through highway is raised several feet above ground level. Twenty yard dirt streets parallel the highway and front the town's stores and houses. I took in the lazy dogs napping on the dirt streets and make my decision. I walked a mile along the empty highway to an old two-story broken adobe building. Chickens flew about several motorcycles in various stages of disassembly in the side yard. Their squawking announced my arrival. The man agreed to patch the tube if I brought the bike. As I returned to retrieve it, the villagers were watching my trek. I was definitely something different for the little town.

The day became fiery hot as I pushed the bike up the slight incline toward the mechanic's garage. Every hundred or so yards I used my hand pump and inflated the tire a little to make the job easier. Sweat, which normally evaporates quickly in Mexico's arid air, did not due to the unusual humidity and soaked my shirt. I was providing more fodder for village conversation than I liked. Halfway there, some young men were working at another tire repair place I hadn't noticed, and they motioned me over. They were about fifty yards off the highway. I debated if the extra walking would be worth it. They wanted to help and insisted on pumping air into the tire. I knew they wouldn't fix the tire, as I was already another villager's customer, so I didn't ask. Pushing became much easier after using their air pump. I only had to work the hand pump once more.

Heat and Exercise

Pushing my motorcycle provides an excellent example of one thing Americans, especially older Americans, should be cautious of in Mexico. The village was located at a high elevation, under a tropical sun, in an arid land. If one walks down the street next to the houses on the sunny side, the temperature is torrid. On the shaded side of the street, the temperature is perfect. While walking the bike on the highway, I had to actually worry about heat stroke. It doesn't seem possible temperatures can vary that much within a few yards, but they will, given the right geographical circumstances.

On this day, I could easily judge the impact of the sun, but that is not always the case. At high elevations, if there's a steady breeze, it's possible to feel cool while exerting yourself. The lack of humidity evaporates perspiration quickly and enhances the sensation of being cool. It's quite possible to never realize you're overheating. Again, common sense must be used in Mexico to avoid these easily-preventable problems.

* * * * *

The motorcycle mechanic was an older gentleman named José Salcido. At first, I wondered if he knew what he was doing. I wasn't used to my bike mechanics running off goats to find a spot for me to sit. He went upstairs for one tool and looked under a chicken nest for another. While we removed the rear tire, neighbors and passerby's stopped to chat about my trip. By the time the tire was changed, the entire village knew José was helping me. Several villagers who had been in the United States came by to say hello. The man refused to take any pay for fixing the tire or even allowing me the privilege of buying him a drink. After many thanks and good-byes, I was off again.

Crossing the rolling green hills was wonderful biking, although there were a few patches of bad road. The scarcity of traffic allowed me to admire the farms and ranches scattered over the hills. I managed to protect my sunburned arms all day. A heavy rain caught me in the late afternoon, ending any worry about the sun.

Arriving in Salamanca, I was surprised to find fifteen or twenty rough-looking joints on the edge of town. It looked like an area that would really rock when the partying started. They weren't open yet, but the people setting up for the evening's activities were helpful and provided directions to get around in the city. I found Hotel El Monte in downtown Salamanca on Juárez, No. 101. The large room, with king size beds and fresh-cut flowers, was reasonably priced.

I walked about Salamanca in the early evening. There are several lovely parks, more or less across from the hotel. They are full of people and life until about 10:30 p.m. when the pedestrians fade into the night. I debated returning to the joints on the edge of town. Instead, I enjoyed a late meal at a local club decorated to resemble an Arabic enclave.

I was seeing more dogs than I'd ever seen in Mexico. Most people still kept their canines on their roofs but now, more were loose in the street. I rarely noticed purebred dogs in Mexico before, but was seeing even the pedigreed breeds. On my first trip through Mexico, I was never once chased by a canine. The reason was simple and would seem cruel to this dog lover, except I've had one run into my motorcycle and cause a crash. If a dog chased a bike, the rider would slowly turn and ride back with his bullwhip and lay the offending animal out in such a manner he lost any further urge to pursue a motorcyclist. It sounds harsh, but the practice probably kept many pets from being run over and many riders from being injured.

I left Salamanca about 7 a.m. The enjoyment of taking the easy curves was offset by cold air over the low mountains. I had to stop three times in the first forty miles to warm up. There were times when the weather was so cold I wished I'd taken the ocean route or had some winter clothes. The country is green and the large hills are pleasing to the eye, but it's really cool in the morning.

11. Morelia-Toluca-Cuernavaca

I made it to Morelia —the capital of Michoacán, considered by many to be the most Indian of the Mexican states— going by and across two large lakes, the Laguna de Yuriria and Laguna de Cuitzeo. Despite a light drizzle, it was rewarding being on the bike. I could pull off anywhere I chose and watch the local people fish. They used patched together wooden boats and, in some areas, men pulled long nets through waist-deep water. Indian restaurants dotted the highway. Black-haired women in neat uniforms served delicious and reasonably priced meals. Fish dominated their menus.

The city of Morelia, at an altitude of 6,235 feet, brings out the worst in Mexican traffic —massive, confusing, snarled, and every man for himself. I loved it. The bike was a part of me and I had the advantages in the morass. Cutting between buses, skimming down a three-foot-wide lane in the traffic, and riding in openings in the opposite lane would be unthinkable in the States, but works perfectly in Mexico. I discovered I had to go to El Centro to reach the Honda shop on Avenida Acueducto. I was not thrilled about going there, as the uncontrolled traffic would slow me, but I was doing fine until I saw the aqueduct.

There was no way to continue driving. I had to stop and see this. I'd been in Morelia several times, but somehow missed the aqueduct. I had to touch it,

47. Honda Service Center in Morelia, 1993.

walk under it, and feel the water seeping down in spots. Standing under a set of its 254, twenty-seven foot-high and eighteen foot-wide arches, I closed my eyes and imagined Roman legions tramping beside it. The aqueduct, built in 1785, is almost two miles long. It's elegant and has a wonderfully inviting walkway beside it. Trees and rich shrubbery intermingle with the buildings on each side of the avenues bordering the aqueduct and mark the beginning of Cuauhté-moc Park. It's almost startling to see such ancient European-style construction in twenty-first century North America.

I had the cycle serviced at the Honda shop called Motos Frame on Av. Acueducto. I wanted to make certain everything was adjusted properly after my flat. A light mist began falling while the bike was being checked. I debated staying and revisiting many of the historic sites in the city, but decided to move on. I traveled thirteen hours, with about three of those in Morelia, and only made two hundred miles. I never

48. Darn if a motorcycle doesn't go well with an aqueduct in Morelia.

saw the sun all day and got caught in a bad situation long after dark, a mistake I do not like to make in Mexico. With the cloud cover, heavy traffic and the rain, visibility became a serious problem. The pockmarked road made a hard right turn, but it was possible to take a left on the curve and travel four miles to the town of Atlacomulco. I went left toward the city but because of heavy rain, flying traffic, bouncing trucks and potholes, I decided even four miles was too dangerous in the dark.

Fortunately, near that intersection was the Hotel Fiesta Mexicana (Carr. Toluca-Atlacomulco Km. 62.5). Rather than try to negotiate the crowded and potholed road in drenching rain and darkness, I decided on the hotel regardless of the price. It was less than seventy dollars, but was absolutely worth every penny, compared to a similarly priced American hotel. A top-quality, large steak, fries and a drink cost about thirty percent less than it would have in the States, and was the best food buy I found in Mexico.

I had a miserable start on the seventh. I had washed my sweatshirt in the bathroom basin before turning in. It felt mighty cold pulling it on wet. I took a long rainy ride from Atlacomulco —about forty miles— to the far side of Toluca. The road is four lanes and busy, with an abundance of potholes. Toluca claims to have the highest elevation of any city in Mexico. From the cold, I'd have believed it even if I didn't know its altitude was 8,900 feet. It's also supposed to be the most industrial and German-like. From what I saw of its industries and rapid pace, I have to agree with that appraisal. I stopped four times due to the cold before reaching Toluca. On my first stop, I put the remains of my poncho between my tee shirt and sweatshirt. It stopped some of the wetness and cold. If I'd left the poncho outside, the wind would have shredded it completely.

My fourth stop was the Holiday Inn on the Mexico City side of Toluca. The road in this section of Toluca is lined with expensive shops and fine restaurants. I chose the Holiday Inn because I'd been looking for stamps and was having difficulty finding a place to purchase them. Mexico doesn't have the best postal system. Stamps are usually available in pharmacies and the lobbies of better hotels. I needed to find some, as I didn't know when I'd be in a large town again. My plan was to take back roads to avoid Mexico City and its massive traffic.

The trip had become a fight to force myself to continue forward. The cold and three days of solid rain took a toll. Still, I wanted to avoid Mexico City and find my way across the big mountains to Cuernavaca and better weather. Everyone in Toluca was wearing heavy sweaters and winter coats except me.

It was even cold in the huge Holiday Inn dining room. I downed coffee and rolls, watching two young

49. But young lovers go even better with the aqueduct in Morelia.

women at another table. Both were wrapped in heavy wool sweaters and sitting on big coats. There was a price to pay for my stubbornness and the poor decision of giving up my jacket. I was hoping to make it to a lower elevation instead of giving in and purchasing a coat. I decided I was the brainchild who didn't pack right. Maybe a few more days of discomfort would teach me a lesson.

After Toluca, the drive was long and harsh. I took poorly-marked back roads that had little traffic and were climbing higher than Toluca's elevation. I stopped often to ask directions in an attempt to reach Cuernavaca. I became lost several times, but enjoyed stopping to find my way back to the correct road. Each time it provided a chance to warm up. My first stop was in a village's two-story adobe country store. An elderly lady was outside making tortillas on a large tin drum. Two men joined her and encouraged me to dry my clothes on the roasting drum. It didn't take long. We passed the time discussing the route and misty weather before I put my now toasty clothes back on. I didn't have a lot of faith in their ideas on the route, as they'd never been to Cuernavaca.

Traveling on, I stopped at low wood-slatted Indian restaurants and warmed myself over wood fires —some of them burning on stone platforms in the middle of dirt floor restaurants. The radio reception and weather reports are better in Mexico than they were just a few years ago. Two Indian women told me why there was so much rain. A hurricane had hit the Acapulco area, causing many deaths. Although I was several hundred miles away, the storm's expanding clouds impeded my ability to drive rapidly or safely. This explained why I been in almost constant rain after my first day in Mexico.

As miserable as I felt at times, I realized a psychological change had occurred. Doctors might claim I'm nuts, but I knew I wouldn't get sick. If the bike breaks down, I'm mentally prepared to make a lean-to and sleep on the ground until I get help. The coolness isn't unbearable, except when riding. Even as I realized I wouldn't get sick, I also knew once I reached Oaxaca I'd better get a hot shower, soup and warm dry clothes fast or when I relaxed, I would become ill.

Soon, even the occasional Indian farm homes disappeared from the landscape. I entered a national park, climbing yet higher in elevation. The heavily forested mountains would have been breathtakingly beautiful in better conditions. Instead, I found them breathtaking for other reasons. I viewed the giant pines through a steady drizzle that increased as I climbed higher. Small rivers and streams gurgled down the highway. Several small landslides and downed trees often blocked the road. Luckily, none of the obstacles proved insurmountable. The narrow

50. A Purepecha fish restaurant on the Laguna de Cuitzeo shore near Morelia.

road lacked guardrails to protect drivers from the sheer drop-offs. I almost slipped off the mountain on one curve. The motorcycle wouldn't respond as I leaned left into the turn. I'd run into a sheet of water flowing over the curve and down the mountainside. Despite my slow speed the bike slid to the right in the oily, streaming water. Strangely, the impending disaster seemed to occur in slow motion. I searched for a limb or clump of shrubs to grip if I kept sliding after I laid the bike down. Thankfully, my forward momentum carried the bike past the rushing sheet of water. I regained traction a fraction of a second before letting the bike go. Despite the terrible weather and obstacles, the lightning was more worrisome than the threat of heavier landslides.

Leaving the national park, I descended rapidly, as many secondary roads emptied into the main highway. After several hours alone in the park, the road became crowded. The flow of traffic to Cuernavaca quickly resembled the pace of a geriatric snail. There

51. Taking a stretch before the final push to Oaxaca.

were absolutely no shoulders. Cars and heavily laden trucks kept the traffic at a near standstill. I was the only person able to occasionally pass. However, even with the bike, it was difficult to pass because of almost endless sharp curves. I had no room in which to squeeze if another vehicle came around a curve. Although it was still raining, my body was warming as I entered Cuernavaca, the city the Shah of Iran settled in when he entered his exile.

It seems nothing changes, despite the people or the time. Cuernavaca was known as Cuauhnahuac before the Spanish arrived, and was the capital of the Tlahuica Indians. The Aztecs conquered the Tlahuica and used Cuernavaca as their ruler's summer residence. The city remains a popular vacation and health resort that attracts not just normal tourists, but the ancient rulers of the Aztec Empire and, recently, a deposed ruler of the modern Persian Empire.

I had not seen a ray of sunshine in two days. I spent the entire day riding slowly and feeling absolutely frozen. In the late afternoon, I stopped long enough to eat a pizza (I still can't get used to pineapple as a topping) and allowed my body to warm a little, then continued south to a town named Cuautla.

12. Oaxaca

Because of the wet, cold and approaching night, I stopped at the Hotel Colonial. It was an excellent choice at less than twenty dollars. It's a Mexican-style hotel with a restaurant and pool. Absolutely everything I had —two pants and three shirts— were soaked. I regretted sending the majority of my clothes back home. I would have had enough if I had kept even half what I sent back. Even a single shirt and pair of pants more would have allowed me something to wear while the others were cleaned.

I walked around Cuautla but my wet clothes were uncomfortable and restricted me. There was a new mall with a large bakery and a department store, among a host of smaller shops, across the street from the hotel. I finally decided to give up my stubbornness and buy a winter jacket, but they had sold out.

While walking and looking at the shops, I passed an elegant restaurant bar. The doorman stepped out and asked, "North American?"

I said yes, and he said, "Tonight you must return and have supper. We have a very excellent club."

I told him I would try. Leaving the modern mall, I browsed the local market until it closed. With nothing to do, I returned to the restaurant bar for supper. Despite the colorful decorations and extensive seating capacity, there were few patrons. The meal, although

52. Monte Albán's ring of pyramids in Oaxaca.

exotic for American tastes, was of Park Avenue quality. I wondered how such places remain open with so little business. The doorman and waiter visited my table often. Both were exceedingly proud of their positions and the restaurant.

Halfway through the meal, a young man and a strikingly beautiful, blond woman entered. The voluptuous lady wore a flowing, blood-red cape and a short skirt, which featured her showgirl's legs. It was hard to take my eyes away from her. It looked as if Al Capp had redrawn Daisy Mae as a city girl. Because a few customers trickled in after her entrance, I thought she must be an entertainer from the Zona Rosa in Mexico City. However, it turned out she was an upper-class woman and the old Mexican rules were in play.

Being strangers, we couldn't just speak directly. Yet, she and the young man had an interest in me, and I in them. The waiter carried a conversation between us from table to table. They learned about my travels. The waiter told me she and her brother were

53. People atop the pyramid at Monte Albán give a sense of perspective.

the owners and were checking on the business. After a few moments of conversation via messenger, it was apparently okay to approach me directly. I'd been somehow introduced. They joined me, and it was great to have the company.

On the eighth, I drove from 10 a.m. to thirty minutes before dark. I was warm for about two hours during the day. The sky threatened rain, but held off except for a few short showers. Sixty miles before Oaxaca, I crossed some fairly high mountains covered with large pine trees heavily draped with Spanish moss. It was an unusual sight. Spanish moss is usually associated with hardwood trees in the American South. In Oaxaca, I found a room four blocks (two down and two over) from the center for about thirteen dollars. It was just what I wanted, spartan and clean.

Two blocks from the hotel was the Superlavanderia Hidalgo, a laundry. It cost five dollars to get nine articles of clothing washed. It was worth it. My clothes were exceptionally dirty from the constant spray of oily highway dirt.

The central square of Oaxaca, the Zócalo, can only be described as exquisite. Its only drawback is that so many American tourists, especially college kids, have

54. Excavations at Monte Albán in Oaxaca and the valley 1,200 feet below.

discovered the setting. Unfortunately, most of them have little idea of the history or culture of the area. The square is magnificent. Its high trees are all painted white for the first four or five feet. The entire area is sealed off to all vehicular traffic.

In the 1960s and '70s, Oaxaca drew American and European hippies wanting hallucinatory highs from its magic mushrooms. It still draws tourists, but today drugs are less of an attraction. Oaxaca is special and, despite the influx of tourists, still has the sense of a magical place with or without its famous mushrooms. The central square is such a magnificent spot even an overabundance of tourists fails to lessen its beauty. Six nights a week there is live music, and I enjoyed a fine orchestra during my meal on the Zócalo.

I shared supper with a young Danish couple making their first visit to the area. We enjoyed a reasonably priced meal and lively conversion. I found it amazing that, despite their European background and having visited many medieval areas, they also found Oaxaca and its architecture fascinating and

55. Monte Albán overlooking the city of Oaxaca — I preferred it when I could motorcycle from pyramid to pyramid.

special. During our conversation, I learned there were several money exchange agencies, called Casas de Cambio, near the center of Oaxaca. A block and a half from Alameda Cathedral was a money exchange that provides a great tourist map to its customers. Eighteen sites and twenty hotels are marked, and it's an excellent aid for a tourist.

The ninth was a long day. I probably should not have stayed an extra day in Oaxaca. I could have ridden four or five hour after visiting Monte Albán. One of the main reasons I went to Oaxaca was to visit the ruins of Monte Albán and motorcycle up the heavily traveled, narrow road that winds to the site. Having driven the road by car years earlier, I'd been thrilled by the tight turns and sheer drop-offs (without guardrails). Holding my breath while giant buses took the inside curves, I prayed they left enough room to allow me by on the outside. The total visual blast of villages, people, animals, scenery and farm life whenever you dared glance away from the road was a thrill I wanted to repeat. I'd dreamed of driving that noodle-like road by motorcycle. As I drove to Monte Albán, my heart broke. I was on a brand new road, not nearly as treacherous or scenic as the old one.

After getting over my disappointment, I enjoyed a three-hour tour of Monte Albán. I had to put up with a host of con men trying to sell artifacts. They had intriguing explanations for how they obtained the ancient treasures. Many of their stone, obsidian and pottery figures appeared authentic, but the pieces were most likely high quality reproductions. Despite the con men, Monte Albán is as mystical as Oaxaca City. In the center of the valley of Oaxaca, a mound climbs 1,200 feet. The ancient Indians leveled the top to build their ceremonial city. The visitor can barely comprehend the work involved. Only the main plaza, 900 by 600 feet, is easily accessible. Surrounding the plaza are 150-foot high pyramids and buildings. Carvings still adorn many of the stone blocks. The view is awe-inspiring when looking at the ring of pyramids, or standing on one of them and taking in the panorama of the valley below.

Gliding down from Monte Albán, I discovered the old road still existed. A short way down the mountain I spotted a right fork that turned out to be the old route to Oaxaca. It's still wonderful for a motorcyclist, but the thrill of the trucks, buses and cars threatening to push you off the mountain curves are missing. There remains only one thing to look out for and that is the road surface. It's now only used by villagers and gets little repair. It appears the army used the surface for artillery practice.

My time in Oaxaca marked the beginning of the end of my trip. Oaxaca is difficult to leave. In fact, many Americans have settled in the area. There was no such possibility for me, despite the attraction.

When I left the United States, my main goal was to visit Oaxaca. If time remained, I'd then venture into the Yucatán peninsula. The trouble with a long trip and being in a foreign country is the boundary of time. I could still go to Yucatán and probably have sufficient time to exit Mexico; but I always make certain I have five free days should an emergency arise. If I traveled to Yucatán, I would use up my emergency days. I had no choice except to return, and that meant another problem. Once I turned northward, the urge to return home has always been like that of a horse given free reign. The trip would quickly become a gallop home. I would skip sites and villages where I might spend days if riding south. Still, I would try to keep my move north at a reasonable pace.

56. Pyramid in El Tajín.

13. Crossing
Cold Mountains to Veracruz

The road from Oaxaca to Tuxtepec and Veracruz leads through high, rugged, pine-covered mountains. The climb in elevation is rapid and the air quickly turns cold and crisp. About twenty miles up the mountain range, I spotted what appeared to be a Swiss chalet, the Restaurant del Monte, on the right.

The little roadhouse looked so inviting I went in and discovered it was built on two levels. Early in the morning, only the lower level was open for business. Each end of the restaurant had a grand fireplace with burning logs providing welcoming and needed warmth for the frigid traveler. Picture windows allowed a view of pine-covered valleys and mountains. The breakfast was deluxe by Mexican standards. Scrambled eggs and slices of canned ham covered a plate that also included a helping of frijoles and a chunk of cheese. Slices of papaya, lettuce, tomato and radishes added further decoration to the plate. A local hot sauce, coffee, side plates of jalapeños and a helping of large tortillas topped off the meal.

I felt sure a German or some European from the Alps had built the place, but I learned ten brothers from Oaxaca opened the restaurant fifteen years earlier and still operate it. The Del Monte sits at over 8,000 feet above sea level and often gets two and

57. A wonderful view of Oaxaca's mountains enhances the meal.

three inches of snow during December and January. When I'm visiting Oaxaca again, I'll definitely drive up to the Del Monte for another meal. The mountain scenery alone is worth a second trip (Km. 27 Carrt. Oaxaca Guelatao).

Refreshed, I left the Del Monte, re-entering the cold air only to climb higher. A light drizzle fell, taking much of the pleasure out of what should have been a wonderful bike ride. The altitude made the ride numbing. I fought the urge to backtrack to Oaxaca and take the route that leads through lower elevations. Finally, I began descending rapidly into a tropical valley. Warmth returned by the mile. Totally recovered within a few minutes, I debated finding a villager to put me up in one of the valley farms. Instead, I decided it was too early and began climbing out of the valley.

The rain fell harder, and the pavement worsened as my bike took me up the mountains. I soon reached points where I climbed through thick cloud cover and was above the drenching rain. I stopped and warmed up in light drizzle, with clouds both below and above. At one point, sixty or so yards above thick clouds, I looked down and it was like viewing a solid object instead of the mist we usually think of as clouds. Sprinkled throughout the Oaxaca side of the mountains were a few primitive Indian restaurants with wooden walls and dirt floors. The owners welcomed me to warm up by their wood fires and served large bowls of hot coffee for about thirty-three cents. Several times I stopped on broad curves where people from remote villages had hiked to catch buses. They spoke Indian languages, but a few knew Spanish. They were always friendly and interested in the motorcycle and where I had come from. The remote area offered the opportunity to achieve an adventure I had in the back of my mind before I left the United States. Unfortunately, I would have needed a combination trail bike to travel into the jungle fastness to see villages and ruins no archaeologist had yet disturbed.

High in the mountains, I spotted an American couple with Missouri plates beside the road and talked with them for a few moments. Once I knew they weren't having car trouble, I left. It felt reassuring to know fellow Americans were following me on such a desolate and primitive road.

I traveled fast, even with streams flowing down the highway and potholes continuously breaking the road. I saw an average of three cars an hour, including the few that passed me. At one of the loneliest spots in the mountains, I stopped and spoke with two Mexicans who had run out of gas. Their car was parked in the middle of the road. Both were drinking heavily, and it was impossible to help them.

The two Americans caught up with me while I was getting the drunks back in their car. They offered the use of a raincoat. I foolishly declined as I was already soaked and mistakenly thought we would soon be out of the mountains. I followed them for at least fifty miles and had little trouble staying directly behind them. The man was a biker and didn't think I could keep up. It was no problem, except in the sections where the pavement disappeared. The road became pure mud for thirty- to fifty-yard stretches, forcing me to creep through at a snail-like pace. Each time I quickly caught them, and we played our game of chase through the horrible conditions. Still, I knew they were on guard for me and I for them.

Finally, the climb stopped and we began descending rapidly. The air warmed and the vegetation became tropical and gigantic "Disney-like" plants with great leaves covered the landscape for several miles. Then, suddenly, we were on flat land. Without consulting a map, I knew I was in the warm state of either Veracruz or Tabasco.

The Missourians and I stopped in the first reasonably sized town in the lowlands and enjoyed a three-hour meal. Together, we shared tales of Mexican travel. They too, had been traveling Mexico and Central America since the early 1970s, purchasing lumber and vacationing. The man, Rico, had not been in Mexico for five years. He was upset over the cost of hotels and food. He expressed surprise when I told him it had been worse a few years before. Accurate maps of Mexico are always difficult to obtain, yet Rico had one from the American Auto Association that was the best I'd seen. I spent part of our dinner studying it, focusing on the areas I planned to explore.

Splitting up from the Americans, I rode through lush tropical land with a wild, green river to my right. Small villages with huts of wood and straw basked in the warm air. The shift from the numbing cold air of

58. Riding above the clouds on the road from Oaxaca to Veracruz. The layer of white cloud cover below looks like a lake.

the mountains was invigorating. I rode with new energy and freedom. I paid more attention to the scenery, as each second was no longer a struggle to keep going.

At the town of Tierra Blanca, I found the El Oasis Hotel for about twenty-three dollars but it wasn't worth it. The office coalesced into the hotel's bar. The place was empty except for an older lady behind the counter, the porter and a young, black-haired beauty having a soft drink at a table. The girl was well dressed and wore white lace covering over her shoulders. I guessed she was the lady's daughter. As the doorman showed me a room, I learned the hotel had rooms with and without hot water.

After paying for my room, I learned the secret of the El Oasis. Despite looking modern, the hotel doubled as a house of prostitution. The owner, an elderly woman, was also the madam. No sooner had I paid, than her manners and facade of respectability faded. She asked if I wanted the young woman sipping the drink. She wasn't pleased with my disinterest.

The hotel was the worst I've stayed in during my years of visiting Mexico, and I'd put up in hotel-brothels before when I'd traveled late into the night. Once I was inside and closed the door, the mildew inside the bathroom quickly permeated the air. The foul odor made it difficult to breathe. I turned off the air conditioner and opened the door so fresh air could clear out some of the stench. The only favorable thing was the room appeared to be clean, mildew aside.

I spent an hour or two on the veranda taking in the night air. I watched several attractive women and a dozen men enter the bar. It was obvious a party of some fever was occurring. Several men asked me to join them. I declined, not out of a fear of the place or trouble from anyone (you can enter this type Mexican house of prostitution and just enjoy the music and a drink), but from a distrust of the madam. From my single stay at this hotel in Tierra Blanca and the fact the town is a major trucking stop, I'd only stay again if I arrived long before dark and checked over the prospective hotel closely. It also made me aware I should still ensure a hotel —even one appearing to be modern— has hot water and air conditioning before renting a room. I don't know how to avoid renting one with such a stench. I had inspected the room before taking it and had smelled nothing.

On July eleventh, I rode from seven in the morning, having not slept well. My first major stop was at Boca del Río, a sleepy little town about ten miles south of Veracruz. Time was becoming a major consideration in planning my return to the States. I disliked the thought of returning, as Boca del Río enchanted me with its riverside walkway and little restaurants.

59. The author poses with a colossal Olmec head in the archaeological site museum at Tres Zapotes, Veracruz.

I wanted to stay for several days, but only walked around for two hours, watching people fish and enjoying the weather. A few retired men strolling along the river walk stopped and chatted for a while, encouraging me to stay and visit in their town. There were three hotels in the little town, but I expect more will soon be built. The best one was Hotel Costa Sol, located on the main highway. Unfortunately, it's not near the grassy, palm-lined walkway beside the inlet. Since 1993, Boca del Río has grown into a large city, merging with Veracruz.

Section IV

1971 - Revisiting the Past

60. North Central Mexico in the early 1970s — miles and miles of open barren land.

14. The Ride to Yucatán

From the Boca de Río-Veracruz area, I wanted to see the Yucatan peninsula. However, before I describe that trip, I want you to step back to 1971 and ride south with me. It was a different Mexico then — rougher, dirtier and more primitive— but one that can still be glimpsed. I've updated the tourist and travel information that has changed over forty-four years, but I encourage you to visit soon, for this Mexico is rapidly disappearing.

I'd been in Mexico for four weeks and had just crossed the mountains from Mexico City to Poza Rica, but I hadn't seen a single American. I'd run across an Austrian on the high desert plains north of Mexico City. It had been my only opportunity to speak English when I helped him reach an airport. Traveling from New York, he'd intended seeing North America and ending his journey in Yucatán. Coming from a mountainous land, the open country of our Southwest had unsettled him but the vast, lonely stretches of Mexico completely unnerved him. His equilibrium was gone. Mentally and physically sick, he needed to return to the congested, urban areas of Europe to regain his bearings. I wasn't as unlucky. I only craved a hamburger and to speak English for a day.

Riding south on the Gulf coast, after Veracruz, my head constantly turned to the left. The water had become a clear, emerald green. The hills rolled down

to ocean, making the ride a series of enjoyable con-
volutions. I'd never seen clear ocean water and the
intensity of the color fascinated me. Luckily, the road
wasn't crowded, allowing me to both ride and gaze.

The ride on Highway 180 was easy. Most of the
towns were small and I found numerous quaint places
to stop for coffee or fruit drinks. (Try the *plátano con
leche*, a banana and creamy canned milk concoction,
if you can find it made the old-fashioned way.) This is
the part of Mexico where women and girls carry goods
balanced on their heads. Although I'd heard of the
practice, the sight fascinated me then and still does.

Prices were low. A bunch of bananas cost a few
cents and bakery delights were cheap. I pulled the
bike onto a side road by a pineapple field. I'd never
seen roadside pineapple sales. For eight cents, the
farmer selected a large one. He quickly skinned and
sliced it with his machete and presented it with a
flourish. Never again has a piece of fruit matched the
sweet succulence I enjoyed that day.

Of course, it wasn't just epicurean delights. Too
often, I'd stop at some seaside village only to have
smiling local men insist I stay a while and enjoy some
rum. It was the first time I'd seen green coconuts
loped off at the top and rum mixed with the fruit's
clear water. It's no wonder so many people think of
leaving the hectic modern world and retiring to a
tropical paradise.

Such pleasantries definitely made it a slow ride.
But the ruins I wanted to see lay buried in jungles to
the south. At Lerdo de Tejada, Highway 180 turns
inland most of the way past Villahermosa. However,
there are a multitude of small roads running back
to the coast. Many of these are worth a ride to see a
Mexico untouched by the tourists traveling to Yucatán. Two of them are a must.

61. There's nothing like motorcycling between small mountains and the ocean north of Veracruz city.

One road leads to the La Venta ruins, often considered the main site of the Olmecs (1300 B.C. to 300 AD), the mother culture of the later Indian civilizations of Mexico and Central America. Most of the statues and artifacts from La Venta, including the massive stone heads, have been moved to Villahermosa and Mexico City. Only the 150-foot high earthen pyramid remains.

The other road leads to Comalcalco, now considered a Maya site. Comalcalco has brick structures and several other archeological features rare or nonexistent in other Indian ruins. Visiting and reading the history of these two sites and civilizations —including much fanciful speculation— is more than worthwhile, but I also enjoy the area for a different purpose.

62. American tourists encountering a Mexican roadside fruit stand.

Running toward the Gulf, the roads are narrow and flat. Cane and jungle crowd the lanes, making the rider feel swallowed by vegetation. Little houses loom through breaks in the thick foliage and a simpler lifestyle blinks forth. Pigs and chickens flutter about mango-shaded huts and kids wave.

63. Boats bob peacefully off the shore of the Campeche coast.

Many of the straw buildings are amazing. I've seen them several times, but always doubt my memory. Straw buildings shouldn't be three stories high and a couple hundred feet long. This is one of those areas I never have enough time for. I re-explore the ruins and try to determine if there have been new excavations or discoveries, but I always have to push on. Someday, I hope to linger and become acquainted with the people of this lowland area.

Taking Highway 180 into Villahermosa is an easy ride. On my first trip, there was something like a bypass around town. I stopped in the street about eight in the morning to retie some equipment. There were few cars to worry about in those days. The baker, the tire repair guy and several other men left their shops and gathered about the bike to talk and see if they could be of help. They insisted I eat before I left and we enjoyed pineapple-filled pastries off the bike seat for an hour while gossiping. The city now has a population of a million, and such a relaxed middle-of-the-street scene isn't possible, but the city remains conducive to motorcycling. Cruising down the lanes next

64. There's nothing like a ferry crossing for a break in 1970s Campeche.

to the river is a pleasure. The La Venta Museum provides a mix of archaeology and nature. Jaguars and crocodiles are among the animals in the jungle-like park. Scattered along the walking paths are thirty-three Olmec sculptures, and a visit to the Hall of Archaeology is worthwhile to see the exhibits on Olmec life.

I headed from Villahermosa on 180 to Ciudad del Carmen and Campeche. Once there were six or seven ferry crossings but, since 1971, bridges have replaced them. I was drowsy riding north toward the Gulf and the town of Frontera when a strange movement startled me. My peripheral vision picked up what can best be described as streaks zipping along the ground. Focusing directly on the spot, I only saw rocks and scrub cactus. About the time I quit wondering about the strange movement, I had to abruptly

65. Think the beach is too crowded today? In Campeche 1971, you could have it all to yourself.

brake. I thought a small child had darted out of the scrub. Startled, I looked and again saw nothing.

A minute later, the odd occurrences were revealed. I was looking ahead at a curve when several lizards rose on their hind legs and started running. I felt a lot better knowing something from the Twilight Zone wasn't stalking me. I'd heard of standing lizards and was pleased to have seen them. However, they continued to startle me when I least expected it.

The coastal road from Frontera to Campeche is still a wonderful ride through an underdeveloped area, but in '71, it was pristine. I hit the first ferry about two hours before dusk. At each subsequent inlet, I had to stop and hope the ferry would return and make one more run. Eight or ten cars and a dilapidated, ninth-class bus also stopped. I talked with a few auto passengers at each crossing. There wasn't a schedule and everyone hoped each ferry would make another trip.

When the ferry docked, we loaded quickly and crossed. As soon as we disembarked, all the vehicles shot out as if they were in the Darlington 500. It was a race to catch the next ferry. Each time, I was off first but quickly lagged behind, especially when darkness fell. The little villages had unmarked *topes,* forcing

66. This is my kind of beach road.

me to go slow to avoid disaster. At the third crossing, the other travelers were rooting for me to make it.

By the fourth crossing, it was jungle dark. Food and drink were available in lantern-lit little shanties built of bamboo, machete-trimmed poles and slats from old packing crates. It was a boggy area, and we had a long wait. The air stilled and the odor of stale swamp water overwhelmed the ocean breeze. Mosquitoes swarmed around the huts. A young mother from the bus huddled her three children together, one breastfeeding, trying to fend off the biting insects. The kids were hungry and crying, and the ravenous insects only made their misery worse. I took my mosquito net from the bike and covered them.

It was an act anyone would have done, but it made me a favorite with the travelers, especially a matronly lady traveling with her daughter and granddaughters. The grandmother told me the woman's husband was in one of the shanties having a drink. I wasn't too smart or inhibited in those days. I went inside and told the guy to buy his kids a drink and to come out and swat mosquitoes. As soon as I touched his shoulder I realized I'd probably done something dangerous.

67. The Cathedral in Merida.

I stepped back and watched for a blade to flash, but the startled man did as I asked. It felt like an eternity before the ferry arrived. A much larger and friendlier reception awaited me at the following crossings.

At the next to last crossing, the passengers had already loaded and actually made the captain wait for my arrival. However, at the last one, my luck failed. I missed the ferry and was trapped on an island between Puerto Real and Ciudad del Carmen. The dockside ferry crew was overly interested in my belongings, so I returned to Carmen. Spotting a brand new soccer stadium on the edge of town, I drove to the middle, spread a blanket and slept like the proverbial baby until dawn.

Awakening early, I found a tattered roadside café and breakfasted on coffee and *frijoles*. I was quickly on my way and rode on blacktop only yards from untouched beaches. There was virtually no traffic to mar the enjoyment of gliding along between the white sand on my left and endless coconut groves on my right. After an hour, I noticed grass huts set about

68. Taking in one of Mérida's historical buildings.

400 yards back in the orchards. I'd probably been passing them all along, but they blended in with the coconut trees and weren't easy to pick out. The ocean breeze made the ride perfect, and I speculated about the lives of the Maya Indians living in those huts. I wanted to stop and find out about these remote people, but I was too new to the country and unsure of my reception.

About ten in the morning, I noticed two Indians walking along the sand. I pulled off and walked down to see what they were doing. The young men resembled statues of Greek gods. Both were perfectly proportioned, with powerful muscles below smooth, bronze skin. It was readily apparent a hard, primitive lifestyle had given them strength modern weight lifters would envy. They carried five-foot long, sharpened sticks for spears. I greeted them, but they spoke neither Spanish nor English. They were friendly and used hand gestures to signal me to follow quietly.

Soon they spotted a fish about fifteen feet from shore. One of the Maya men slowly waded into the

69. Outside the Mérida Market.

water. I couldn't believe my eyes. He literally crept up on the fish, then lifted his rough-hewn spear, threw and raised a three-foot fish from the water. They used their heels to scoop a shallow hole in the sand at the water's edge, then tumbled the fish in and covered it to keep it fresh, before walking on in search of another.

After Campeche, the road turns inland to Mérida. It was interior Yucatán hot and the ride was uneventful, except for encountering two French hitchhikers. They were sitting beside the road next to a patch of stubby shrub cactus. I stopped to get information. One asked in English, "Water please."

They were dehydrated from the sun. In those days, it was necessary to treat water with halazone tablets to purify it. Unsteady and weak, the thirsty men were beyond the point of caring about the water's safety. Thankfully, I had treated water and allowed them all they could drink. Once they recovered a bit, I rode on with an empty canteen, but knowing they'd catch a bus or produce truck before too much longer.

70. A part of Yucataán's Dzibilchaltún archaeological site.

Like most people, I loved the city of Mérida at first sight. The hotel and fancy restaurant row didn't yet exist. Instead, the multi-storied mansions and walled homes were still residences that weren't always exclusively the abodes of the rich. The street was mixed with wealthy homes and buildings used for multiple dwellings. In the early evening, a Caribbean atmosphere prevailed over the more traditional Mexican culture. Clubs opened just off the square and a mixture of American and hot-Latin music rumbled from doorways where shapely Maya girls waved, urging people to enter this or that dancehall.

I would have enjoyed staying in Mérida, but needed a smaller, less hectic base from which to see the ruins. I went about twenty miles to Progreso. It was and is a wonderful little beach town. Today, at the end of the beach road, is a small settlement of American and Canadian retirees. In '71, it was entirely Mexican except for a single American restaurateur who had settled there with his wife and daughter. I was glad to run into them. I was able to get my fill of hearing

71. Cows grazing at the ruins in Dzibilchaltún.

English and enjoy something close to an American hamburger. They, too, were glad to see another American. The man had a Honda 450 out front. It was the first bike I'd seen in Mexico larger than my SL 175. I thought someone had finally made southern Mexico on a large street bike, but he quickly destroyed that notion. He'd returned to the States for the motorcycle however, south of Veracruz, realized the roads would ruin it. He found someone to truck it south.

Deciding to explore the Dzibilchaltún ruins, I headed a few miles south of Progreso. After about three miles, I noticed a road to the right running between two lagoons and decided to take a side trip. The road quickly turned into a sandy lane, then hit the coast and slowly curved south. I passed through two villages of a few thousand people each, until arriving at one named Extoul. Entering town, I passed a long palm frond-covered bar and fishing establishment on the right. The tiny village was built around a treeless, sand square the size of a city block. The only vehicle in town was a rust-red, broken-down, ten-ton

72. The front yard of my Extoul abode.

truck. The ancient truck was parked off the square next to a circus/carnival that took up about a fifth of the square. I rumbled around the single, broad, sandy village street a couple of times before deciding on a kitchen cabinet-sized restaurant on the far side of the square.

I sat at the first of two tables. The *señora*, young girls and children tending the rarely used establishment appeared excited, fearful, amazed and welcoming all at once. While I stumbled through my newly acquired Spanish, establishing they had no menu, villagers walked slowly by the Honda 175. The Maya are a shy people until you get to know them. No one came closer than ten feet from the bike.

I finally stammered out an order for a ham sandwich and a cup of coffee, and the activity really picked up. The *señora* barked her orders. Children and young girls flew from the restaurant. It was before refrigeration and these isolated people were poor. The kids reconnoitered in the few other eating establishments gathering two pieces of bread at this one,

73. Inside a government building in Merida.

a slice of ham from the one with ice that day, lettuce from another and a jar of Nescafé from yet another. It appeared I was that week's entire business. Serving me was a complex undertaking.

The townspeople sent for a young man named Bela. He'd been working for a Louisiana man who owned a chain of sporting goods stores, and was home on vacation. I was surprised at his height and slim build, but later discovered the Maya in this area are taller than most. Bela spoke a fair amount of English, and was friendly and helpful. He showed me around town and encouraged me to stay at an abandoned hacienda on a nearby coconut plantation.

Bela jumped on the back of the bike and we rode a quarter mile from the village to a spot with nothing but thousands of coconut palms and the hacienda. Much of the roof was gone, but a single windowless, roofed room fifty feet from the beach was perfect for my needs. I set up my hammock and had a rent-free home in Yucatán to return to for many years.

Except for their small fishing boats, the sparse

74.
Outside
the
Mérida
market
in 1971.

equipment I carried on the bike was far more than any family in the village owned. Yet in all my time there and during subsequent visits, I could leave my clothes and equipment unattended, knowing no one would steal or bother a single item. With Bela's friendship, I was quickly accepted in the everyday flow of village life. I'd go to various ruins, Progreso or Mérida during the day and return around dusk for the comradeship of my new friends.

One afternoon, I was surprised when two young boys ran down to the beach and urged me to return to the village. I couldn't understand anything more than Bela had sent for me. I jumped on the bike and headed for the square. Bela was sitting with an American couple. They had heard another American was in the area and motorcycled over to say hello.

They were about my age and we spent several hours talking and riding along the beach. They had ridden from San Francisco to Yucatán on what I've come to consider the greatest, dollar-for-dollar, all-purpose motorcycle ever built. They had two tiny Honda 90s. After getting over the shock of seeing what they'd ridden, I compared our bikes. People had kidded me about the small SL 175. I figured they'd have had a stroke contemplating Mexico on a Honda 90. I'd spent close to $800 for the SL 175. They'd bought two Honda 90s for about the same price. I could cruise at about 45 mph and them at 35 mph. They got 128 miles per gallon to my 64. Most amazing, each of their bikes carried more equipment than mine. They'd ridden down the Baja when the road wasn't paved. Painted rocks or cactus were often the only markers signifying they were actually on the route. At dusk, they had to return to their lodging in Mérida. I told them about the ruins at Uxmal and they planned to head that way. As they rode off, I realized they'd had a ride and an adventure I'd always envy. I'd never find the time or money to ride the Baja before it was paved.

The large village square was used for all-day baseball games. Their equipment looked like discards from a depression era, minor-league ball club. However, the continuous games produced talented players. The villagers were exceedingly proud they'd recently beaten a team touring from Mexico City.

The other topic of village conversation centered on the traveling circus/carnival. It had arrived six weeks earlier but ran out of money when their truck broke down. Every day, two hours before dark, the little troupe would set up for the evening performance. At dark, two or three villagers would have enough cash to attend. I left before the troupe earned enough to fix their truck and have often wondered how long it took them to get on the road again.

Bela and I spent many evenings sipping drinks and visiting the owner of the palm frond-covered bar and fishing establishment on the edge of town. The proprietor had little business until American hunters and fishermen returned to the area. One afternoon, at about 1 p.m., I made the mistake of deciding to eat there. I was particularly hungry, but the day wore on and on the owner assured me every so often the meal would soon be ready. I was served shortly before dark. It was then I discovered his son had literally put to sea to find my fish. It was tasty and definitely had no relationship to today's fast food franchises in quality or promptness.

* * * * *

For many years I always found my windowless, seaside room waiting when I visited Extoul. Then I started traveling more in central Mexico and didn't visit for eight years. When I returned, modernity and the flip side of the Cancún beach-front development had occurred. Mexicans had adopted the American dream of having a beach home. Prices were prohibitive on the Cancún side of Yucatán, but land in this area on the Gulf remained inexpensive. The sandy road was now a paved lane. Instead of seaside jungle, a jumble of poorly constructed beach shanties lined the way. The first two small villages had become good-sized towns. My little village had grown to eight or ten thousand. My coconut grove and the old broken hacienda had been plowed under to make way for new development. I found a few of my Maya friends, but the village was now predominately Mexican.

15. Beating the Packaged Tourists to the Mexican Riviera

It was difficult leaving the Progreso-Mérida area, but I had other ruins to see. Beyond a few trucks, there was little traffic in 1971 Yucatán. I rode slowly and poked around as I drove. About an hour from Merida, I found the road to Izamal. It's referred to as the Yellow City, as most of its buildings are painted that color. I wanted to visit, as I'd read the tallest pyramid in Yucatan was there. The ride was along a narrow lane surrounded by thick foliage. Occasionally, limbs stuck out over the highway. I felt as if I was traversing a road to nowhere when suddenly, I was in the little city of Izamal.

I kept circling the town, always looking away from the city to spot the pyramid, but spiraling closer to the center. I stopped at a line of two story houses on one side of the street and little wooden soda, candy, tobacco shops, and *fruterías* on the other. I gave up trying to spot the pyramid. I sat at one of the shacks for a drink and asked the vendor for directions to the pyramid.

With a surprised look, he said, "Just go behind my store."

I walked the narrow slit between the thirty-foot deep shops. Bright sunlight and sweet green tree branches loomed at the end of the dark alleyway. I

75. Since 1971, a stone staircase has been added to the pyramid at Izamal.

76. A buddy stops to rest on first level of the Izamal pyramid.

77. The first pyramid level and the town of Izamal below.

thought I was going to enter a little jungle but, when I stepped into the light, there were only a few trees at the base of a monstrous, grass-covered, earthen mound. I looked upward at the pyramid. It was big and apparently undisturbed. The line of stores had blocked my vision. Still, I felt like a fool having been unable to spot the pyramid from only thirty yards away.

A narrow cow path meandered at an angle toward the top. I climbed up, following the worn trail and avoiding steaming cow pies. On leaving the shade of the little trees, the humid subtropical heat became oppressive. I was soaked before reaching the top. But I was in for a surprise. I hadn't reached the top at all. Instead, I stood on a huge, grass-covered plateau. Several hundred feet ahead lay the upper part of the pyramid.

It was still hot, but a gentle breeze on the plateau helped. I hiked over and began climbing the narrow steps. The wind increased as I climbed, until I reached the final surprise. Yet another pyramid wait-

78. The author taking a break while climbing Izamal pyramid second level in 2003.

ed on this tier. Comfortable in the breeze, I climbed once again, wondering if yet another pyramid loomed. However, I was on the last one but it rewarded me with a panoramic view. The colonial city, gleaming yellow, and the great monastery contrasted sharply with the surrounding ocean of green jungle. I basked in a cool wind I wished could follow me back to the heat and humidity waiting below.

From Izamal, Chichén Itzá beckoned. The interior Yucatán jungle was sixty- and seventy-foot high crowded brambles. It wasn't what I thought of as jungle, but I'd have hated trying to cut my way through such dense vegetation. Little villages sliced off the highway every few miles, but I didn't see any type of lodging. I debated visiting one of the little villages, but feared neither Spanish nor English would be spoken, when I spotted a clearing where a Pemex gas station was under construction. I pulled in and found a squat, old Maya man on guard duty. He helped me pull a few planks together to make a bed off the floor

79. The top of the Izamal pyramid. Note the size of the second tier base.

next to his hammock. The smell of concrete dust permeated the building, but it didn't prevent my sleeping soundly until the morning sun stirred me. The old man had a fire going and a crude, coffee-like drink boiling. I've never known what it was, but it certainly jump-started my morning.

Chichén Itzá was different than can be easily imagined by today's visitors. The highway cut directly through the ruin. Beyond a single Maya worker, not a person —tourist or otherwise— visited the archeological zone the entire day. A tiny fruit stand just past the ruin was the only business to serve the few passing motorists.

I rode the bike from structure to structure, marveling at the work and history. This was the city that —along with Tula, north of Mexico City— played such an important role in the conquest of Mexico. Around 800 AD, there had been a revolt among the Toltecs in Tula. Their bearded, white god, Quetzalcoatl (known

80. The streets of Izamal.

as Kukulcán in Mayan) left Tula with half the tribe. They traveled 1,500 miles and conquered the people living at what we call Chichén Itzá. Part of Chichén Itzá is a copy of Tula. An Indian myth in Central Mexico predicted the white or bearded god would return in the year 1519. Amazingly, that was the year Hernán Cortés landed, and many Indians thought he was the returning god.

It was easy to tell which structures and carvings were Toltec. Human skulls and horrific carvings of combat in part of the site demonstrate the Toltec influence. Based on the art and number of sacrificial victims, many archeologists believe the Mayan people practiced human sacrifice on a smaller scale than the civilizations of Central Mexico. Today, it takes a long, hard day to tour Chichén Itzá but that wasn't the case in 1971. I motorcycled from structure to structure and was able to climb and study each structure individually.

Near Chichén Itzá is the city of Valladolid. The little town is noted for its many cenotes. One cave-

81. The Observatory at Chichén Itzá.

like cenote just outside of town is now being promoted for tourists. It is no longer as rewarding a visit as was the case when only Indians, local farmers and the occasional lucky tourist hearing of it visited. That cenote was one of the most fantastic places I'd ever seen. The entrance was a small break in the sandstone surface. A narrow, slippery, stone path, traveled by Mayans for untold thousands of years, meandered down through the darkest twilight until reaching the bottom ledge. A shaft of light cut through a hole in the earth perhaps eighty feet above the cavern. The center of the pool basked in bright daylight while the light's strength faded around the cave. The habit was to go along with the natives, strip to your underwear and plunge into the blue water for a wonderful swim.

Unfortunately, making the cenote a tourist draw erased the magic once associated with the site. A string of electric lights brighten the cavern too much. Many of the stalagmites have been damaged. However, the locals still use the cavern for bathing and swimming. Fortunately, Valladolid offers other cenotes that have

82. The cenote at Valladolid.

retained all their wonder and charm. One of the best is in the center of town and has a great restaurant sitting above it.

I foolishly left Chichén Itzá at dark, headed for Isla Mujeres, now part of the Maya Riviera. The ride took a creepy six-hours. I felt as if I were shoulder to shoulder with the encroaching jungle. My headlight provided the only light, and I didn't pass a single vehicle. The beam awakened unknown jungle birds warming themselves on the highway. Flapping large wings, they quickly disappeared in the dark night. Every now and then, I spotted flashes of yellow through the jungle fastness. The glimpses of wavering yellow added to the eeriness of the ride. I couldn't imagine lightning bugs large enough to blink such a light through the jungle. After hours alone, thoughts of vampires with glowing eyes filled my thoughts. I finally stopped at a clearing beside the highway and realized the yellow illuminations were candles or lantern wicks flickering in the wood-slat and pole Maya homes.

83. View of the Valladolid cenote from the back wall.

I finally reached the villages on the Caribbean Sea. There was nothing open. No lights shone in any of the darkened houses. I found the seashore and drove onto the sand. It would be my bed for the evening.

I awoke to the clearest blue sea I'd ever imagined. I had been taken with the clear, green water of the Gulf. However, this sparkling blue made the Gulf water seem dull and listless. The area was primitive, but the coconut groves against the sparkling sea made it an inviting spot. A quick ride around the tiny towns indicated not much was going on. I expect there was a hotel of some sort, but I never spotted it. It would be several hours before a launch departed for Isla Mujeres. I'd heard there were sky-high hippies running around nude on Isla Mujeres, but I didn't think viewing high hippies was worth the wait. Instead, I headed south on the coastal road.

Today, it's about an hour's ride from Cancún to Tulum. In 1971, the road was so pockmarked and broken it took six hours on a combination bike. I inched forward, crisscrossing the road constantly in an effort to avoid holes and stay on higher and more complete pieces of broken pavement. The only vehicle I encountered was a broken-down Mercedes bus. A group of complaining German and French tourists, gripped in complete misery, huddled in a foot-wide patch of shade next to the vehicle. They'd been stuck for two hours. They were soaked in perspiration and none had been prepared for the heat and humidity. The driver said a truck was coming to tow them. I couldn't help, so I eased on in first gear, searching for the rare opportunity to shift to second.

I ate lunch at a bright-blue roadside stand outside a little Maya village. I was an object of curiosity as people studied my white skin and features. I believe they were more fascinated with my strangeness than with the bike. I'd already seen the beauty of many Maya women, but this little tacked-together stand had one of the best behind the counter. As I ate pineapple slices and drank a *plátano con leche,* the young woman nursed her baby. She was a true knockout. Her embroidered muslin shift revealed curves that reminded me of Lana Turner playing a role in a slip. She attempted a conversation in broken Spanish, but it was quickly apparent she only knew a few words and sentences. I left quickly, realizing this flirting seventeen-year-old would either lead to a divorce or me being taken apart by a jealous husband wielding a machete.

I expected a town when I reached Tulum, and was disappointed only on that point. A wooden store built off the ground and a numerous frond-covered homes spread out amid a coconut grove comprised the village. A half a mile away was a British commune. The inviting little settlement made me want to linger, but the storeowner said the Federales would

84. The Quintana Roo coast near Tulum was still deserted in 1978, with virgin beaches and crystalline waters.

Photo by Mark Brennecke

soon raid the commune for their drug use. I figured with my fair skin, I'd get hauled off if I was around. I needed gas to reach Chetumal. The owner said the next Pemex was in Chetumal, but he had some five-gallon cans. There was no way to measure out what I needed and I was forced to buy all five gallons to get a little over one gallon.

With regret at not being able to spend time in Tulum, I left, hoping to find a suitable place to spend the night. The road was brand new and the best I'd been on. I drove fast until I hit a three foot dip across the highway. Thank heavens I had the facemask down. My face slammed down onto the handlebars, but somehow I kept the bike upright as I braked hard. With the sun's reflection, I couldn't see the paved ditch in the light gray pavement. The resulting jolt suddenly had me again driving extra-safely after I

85. Typical Maya home in the Yucatán countryside in 1971.

walked around a while and made sure I'd not broken
any teeth, ribs or other bones.

I got lucky an hour before dark. Three Maya
men in tattered, button-less shirts squatted next to
a small clearing off the highway enjoying a smoke. I
pulled over and discovered one spoke Spanish. They
were highway workers left to chop weeds and bram-
ble with machetes. They welcomed me to bunk with
them. With the last rays of sun, I walked the bike behind them through a few hundred feet of jungle and
into the rubble of ancient ruins until we reached their
hut. It was an oval building with brown, two-inch by
nine-foot tall saplings for walls. The threshold lacked
a door and the roof was thatched with palm fronds.
I was allotted the hammock closest to the entrance.

The men quickly snuffed their candle. The night

86. A Yucatecan Maya home with its trypical thatched roof.

was black but I could make out darker forms through
the doorway. Although I had no apprehension, it
crossed my mind if these strangers murdered me, no
one would know for a long time —and no one would
have a clue where I'd been killed. I listened to the
insects and nighttime animals while swaying in my
hammock. The dark shapes outside quickly faded
with the oblivion of sleep.

Sometime, late in the night, I awoke to one of
the most memorable experiences of my life. I stared
through the door in amazement. For several minutes, I thought I was dreaming. The looming night
forms were gone, and I stared up at the silhouette of
a Maya temple outlined by a giant, yellow moon. It
was so bright I could see into the jungle and make out
branches. The piles of rubble with trees growing out

of them were more detailed than when we'd walked to the hut. I focused on the largest pile and followed it up. Branches of great trees crossed part of my view, but my eyes continued, past the tree level, to where the surviving structure of the temple reached a hundred feet into the sky. Such imposing structures must have amazed the ancients. This one certainly captivated me. Had I been raised in this ocean of jungle, I would have been certain only the gods could have been responsible for such an edifice. My short view was timeless. I could have been looking from 1,500 years ago. I felt I'd been allowed a special privilege and lay gazing at the incredible moonlit sight until the sleep I no longer sought again captured me.

The Maya men were already up and cooking when I awoke. We squatted in front of the hut to eat. We enjoyed coffee —made from boiling grounds and straining the liquid— and tortillas stuffed with some kind of meat. I studied the ruin I'd seen during the night. It was no longer as magnificent and awe inspiring, just marvelous. Heaps of broken rock, tumbled boulders and centuries of collected dirt made up its base. Six or eight feet up, large trees began growing out of it. They rose perhaps seventy feet, until the top of the pyramid/temple broke the tree line. It was gray and dank in the morning light. It was still impressive, but it had lost the glory and magic the full moon had bestowed upon it.

Later, I followed the Maya men to a small cenote hidden in the jungle. They pointed out a few trees crisscrossed with old slice marks. They were sapodilla trees, the species that provided the sap for chewing gum. Despite the coal black water, we stripped down. I watched my companions enter the cenote before following. It was a refreshing bath, but cold as the dickens when we emerged.

I made my way to the free city of Chetumal. In two days, I hadn't seen a vehicle on the highway besides the broken-down bus. Lacking the import duties restricting Mexican development, Chetumal, bordering British Honduras —now Belize— was a different world. Motorcycles and cars of every type zipped along through the steamy tropical heat. The stores carried far more goods than could be found in Mexico. The people were friendly and helpful. A guy on a blue Honda 360 directed me to a hotel, a hundred year-old, wood building. I trooped up the narrow stairs to check out the room. Despite the dark, dank hallway, I was particularly delighted when the door opened. I guessed the furniture and fixtures could have been prized museum exhibits, except the rooms had functioning window mounted air-conditioning units.

It was tempting to linger in Chetumal a few days just to enjoy the benefits of air-conditioning. Instead, I had to head for home and re-entered the scarcity of feudal Mexico during the early afternoon of the following day. Highway 186 was new and even better than the road south of Tulum. It must have been well constructed, for even today, it remains in good condition. There was little traffic and I saw virtually no towns for 200 miles. I rode slowly, enjoying the land and empty highway.

At the ruins of Xpujil, serious excavation had just started. The lone caretaker spent the late afternoon showing me the few rooms that had been uncovered. While he showed me a carved stone, a large iguana made the mistake of darting into some bushes. I helped the caretaker catch the big, green lizard. I left with the sun setting and the caretaker happy he had fresh meat for his family's supper.

The road was lonely during the afternoon. As darkness closed in, I longed to see any village, hut, or

87. There were no other visitors in Tulum on this day in 1978.

passing motorist. There was little hope of that. Only three vehicles had gone by all day. At dusk, I cut on my lights. Within a minute, the bike died. I fumbled with the gas switch, puzzled why I needed the auxiliary tank so soon. It wasn't the gas. I spotted a clearing on the edge of the jungle and glided onto a rock-covered area highway crews used to turn around.

No sooner had I dismounted and read through the repair manual, than it was totally dark —as if someone had switched off the lights in an interior room. The murmur of the jungle quickly grew to a ferocious roar. I was certain I heard jaguars. I tried to convince myself it was howler monkeys and other jungle life with smaller appetites, but it did no good. I was satisfied at least one of the big cats was prowling just out of sight.

I flicked my Zippo to examine the fuses. Mexicans had rarely seen cigarette lighters. The wonderful invention had amazed and entertained them. It was a land where matches were more expensive than cigarettes. The cost of a lighter was prohibitive to all but

88. The lonely seaside fortress at Tulum in 1978 before the coast was developed.

Photo by Mark Brennecke

the wealthiest. Yet, such reflections didn't cross my mind as I fumbled with the bike's side panel. If I had to spend the night, would pulling the bike over me be any protection if a killer cat came? Would the Zippo's flame keep a hungry feline at bay?

There it was. The flickering flame showed the fuse's filament cleanly burnt through. Holy Jesus, that roar sounded close. What a damn coward I was. I ran my shaky fingers along the wires and worked them loose. When I touched them directly, a shaft of light cut the clearing and lit the dark foliage. I'd forgotten to click the lights off. The beam brought both hope and the realization of how truly isolated I was. The lit section of vegetation appeared even more ominous. I quickly mounted and kicked the bike into a roar. I hoped the noise would scare any animal away, at least for a while. I dismounted and nervously gath-

ered the gear I'd taken out. I hurriedly stuffed it anywhere it wouldn't fall out. Proper packing could wait.
Right then I wanted to escape the little clearing.

Back on the road, it was impossible to drive
without lights. Reluctantly, I left them on, hoping
my jury-rigging wouldn't cause too much damage. I
rode, still nervous and far more aware of how remote
an area I was traveling through. Even the moving
bike didn't provide the security I wanted at the moment. It was silly to speculate about a jaguar taking a
man off a moving bike but, once nervous, such idiotic
thoughts lingered. I prayed the lights wouldn't fail
before I found a town.

An hour later, I reached a closed Pemex station at
a T junction on the highway. A sign indicated a town
or village twenty kilometers down the side road. The
building was brand new, and no one was around. I'd
shaken my uneasy feeling and decided to sleep next
to the station wall. I don't think I'd fully stretched out
on the concrete walk before I fell dead asleep.

The strained coughing of the sickest dog I've ever
seen woke me at dawn. I looked to make certain it
wasn't foaming at the mouth. Thirty yards past the
hacking brown canine, seven Maya highway workers squatted around a small fire. They smiled and
waved me over.

They were heating something in a half-gallon
tin can. Through sign language, they signaled me
to get a cup from my gear. I squatted next to them
by the fire and enjoyed the heat in the early morning coolness. It was amazing it could be so cool. In
less than two hours, the temperature would be pushing 100 degrees Fahrenheit. One of the men scooped
some strange-looking greenish, sticky gruel into my
cup. As I studied the syrupy contents of the steaming
broth, the men pointed and repeated, "*Maíz. Maíz.*"

89. A rustic store in Tulum in 1978. Photo by Mark Brennecke

It was a corn preparation. As wheat is the staff of life to us, the Maya say corn is life. It looked alien with stringy swirls in the broth, but I spooned a mouthful. It was delicious. It may as well have been rich, chicken noodle soup. With each spoonful, I sensed it was nourishment I needed. During my second cupful one of the men shook my shoulder and pointed.

A pickup carrying the station's owner and his nineteen-year-old daughter pulled onto the lot. The young woman spoke some English. They were upper-class people from Mexico City. She was far better educated than virtually anyone within a hundred miles. They encouraged me to explore the local area. I was surprised at the father's reaction. I don't think the invitation was because I was swell, but that the young woman probably had no social life. Mexico was and remains a highly stratified society. The daughter had virtually no one to freely interact with. It was obvious the father had gotten the only Pemex concession in the area and would make a fortune. I guessed it was

90. The Temple of the Inscriptions is perhaps the most important in Palenque.

rare to find anyone nearby who had read a book or approached the social level of this father and daughter. It was in his interest to keep me around, lest his daughter go batty. In 1971, not a single village marked the map on this 150-mile stretch of highway. My current map shows only one.

I talked with them for over two hours, until the first customer arrived. Then I was off. When Highway 186 West dead-ended into Highway 186 North/South, I turned left and headed south to Palenque. The road through the town of Palenque was dusty, but it quickly wound up into the tropical highlands. Horses tied near vaqueros cutting brush startled at the passing bike. The cowboys waved their great straw hats and machetes in a friendly greeting. Suddenly, I was amid the glorious and mysterious Palenque ruins.

The few workers at the site hadn't seen a tourist

91. The archaeological site of Palenque in Chiapas.

for weeks. I rode from edifice to edifice and even up some of the less steep steps. The workers were glad to see a stranger. A fellow hanging around took the time to show me various parts of the ruins. There was no problem entering the Temple of Inscriptions and looking around. The fellow with me worried I might fall as we walked down to the dark tomb. Ironically, at the time, there was more interest in the arch being closest to a true arch in the New World than the sarcophagus lid of Maya ruler K'inich Janaab' *Pakal*. Eventually, the lone archeologist showed up and gave me the history of the site. I spent the night with two workers who rigged up a piece of canvas for a shelter beside one of the smaller ruins.

The next morning, I left Palenque and rode twenty or thirty miles toward San Cristobal de la Casas, which is on Highway 199 off of 186. I wouldn't have time to cross the high mountains, but I wanted to see the little river I'd heard about. The road was a series of roller coaster hills, particularly enjoyable for motorcycling. I pulled off the highway and glided down onto a grassy meadow next to Cascadas de Agua Azul.

Oh, my lord, the scenery captivated. Clear, clean water tumbled down a series of natural steps. A riverbed of white sand and sandstone gleamed up through tide-blue water. I had the wonderful spot all to myself. The sweet scent of wild flowers growing everywhere in this natural garden filled my nostrils and bird songs filled the air. An occasional truck rumbled by, interrupting nature's symphony. I wished a local was about so I could ask if there were any snakes or alligators. However, I was alone in this remnant of paradise.

The water flowed so transparent I could clearly see the bottom. The only places anything could be hidden were at spots along the shore where long, slim-leafed plants floated in the rapid flow. I found a spot where nothing covered the banks, grabbed my soap and stripped to my underwear.

Talk about heaven. I sat in two-feet of sparkling water, relaxed and bathed. I didn't want to quit lounging but forced myself to wash my dirty clothes. Soon, my bike was covered with wet clothes flapping from the handlebars and hanging from every other part of the machine. I lazily soaked for another hour allowing my clothes to dry. I'd trail them off the bike when I mounted again, to dry them completely.

The exit off 186 had definitely been worth the detour. I'd dallied too long, but still hoped I could make Villahermosa before dark. I picked up a fifteen-year-old Mexican kid waiting for a bus, and was glad to have the companionship. About two hours before dark, we cut through an area of marsh and streams and were hit by flying insects. The half-inch to two-inch critters were pelting us and the bike like driven hail. I had to stop several times to clean squished insects from the helmet's mask. That wasn't so bad but, when live ones got into my clothes, it was disconcert-

92. A typical Mayan home in 1971 located right on a highway in Yucatán.

ing to feel them struggling against my bare skin.

It was dark when we finally passed through the swarm but, even worse, my headlamp quit working. We inched through the night into Villahermosa. The kid knew a yard mechanic in his neighborhood. I didn't like the guy, but we rolled the bike into a side garage and he quickly had the wiring exposed. Unfortunately, most of the insulation had fused together. It was obvious this mechanic was experimenting. I wouldn't let him do everything he wanted, but he did figure out a way to get a live wire to the headlamp.

With only a headlight, I found my way back to the highway and a hotel. I felt uneasy driving without taillights or a turn signal, but knew I wouldn't be ticketed. I wondered if I could avoid a ticket in the States by buying a blinking, battery-operated light to tie to the back.

I went to bed dispirited, but the morning sunshine made life look much better. I rode up the coast, concerned about the bike and the half-baked repair job. At the town of Minatitlan, I stopped at a cantina and asked some people where I could find a good bike mechanic. Mexicans use the word *maestro* to indicate someone with great expertise. That was how they termed this mechanic.

At his little shop, I knew I was with a *maestro* within minutes. He lacked the parts to fix everything, unless I could wait for him to order them. I couldn't, so he expertly separated what wires he could, located the worst shorts and rapidly fixed them so a fuse could again be used. When he finished, I was still without turn signals and taillights, but I was confident the headlights would continue working. He would only take enough money to cover the new fuse, but did allow me to buy him a couple of beers. I reached Veracruz late that afternoon and found a beachfront room.

Section V

Finishing the Ride

93. Government building in Veracruz.

16. Leaving 1971
for Today's Veracruz

It was time to return to the present. I hated to stop my reflections of my 1971 trip, but I had to get going. I took a last look at the shady Boca del Río riverside walk, got on my bike and started the few miles to Veracruz. The landscape approaching the city had changed greatly in just a few years. Instead of open land and ocean to the east, big business had moved in. Large hotels, condos and modern buildings blocked much of the view. I ignored them and headed down the *malecón* referred to locally as "the Boulevard."

Only one multi-story hotel had moved onto the original beach strip. It was still the old hot, humid Veracruz except along the beach, where ocean breeze provided a bit of respite. Most guidebooks don't acknowledge Veracruz —the first European city built on the mainland of the Americas— as having a lot of attractions. I, however, find the city intriguing. I slowly motorcycled around, enjoying the architecture of the colorful municipal buildings. It was a day of zipping here and there, then back to a restaurant along the beach and finally a visit San Juan de Ulúa.

Once again, Mexico carried me back in time. My American mind wondered for the thousandth time at the fact medieval Europe could be so close to our country. The great fortress of San Juan de Ulúa, be-

94. I believe the walls of the old fort ar San Juan de Ulúa could still withstand a pretty good hit.

gun in 1535, was well worth my afternoon. It was built on an island overlooking the seaport as a defense against buccaneers. The freedom to roam the fort had me feeling like a boy in minutes. Thankfully, the heat ensured I didn't jump from ramparts or try enacting any other boyhood dreams. The fort is constructed from coral cut into great blocks. The ocean breeze made the shady parts of the fort comfortable, but more surprising was the coolness in the interior rooms. San Juan de Ulúa was turned into a prison in the nineteenth century. One can barely imagine men survived hanging by their arms in the dungeons much less many of the other tortures routinely employed.

In the afternoon I returned to the beach and ran across a restaurant flying a Confederate flag. It turned out to be an excellent steak house, filled with a hard drinking crowd enjoying a rock band. I needed to go no further to enjoy a lively last night in Veracruz.

Heading north the next morning, I discovered the

95. San Juan de Ulúa is still protecting the city of Veracruz.

area around and north of Veracruz City had grown tremendously. With it, the roads had changed significantly, making it confusing to pass through the outskirts. Going through town, five motorcycle cops signaled me over. I'm always nervous when pulled in the States, but even more so in Mexico. My worries about being shaken down or hassled faded quickly. They quit monitoring traffic and we discussed bikes for half an hour. They had older Harleys and were interested in how the Honda had held up. Looking at the pockmarked city road, I well understood why they wanted information on the bike's durability.

Getting good directions, I left the officers and rode north to Cempoala, (sometimes spelled Zempoala). The new road bypasses many of the pueblos it went through a few years earlier, but the village is still just off Federal Highway 180 (where Hernán Cortés raised the first Christian cross on the mainland of the New World in 1519). Cempoala has long been one of my favorite Mexican villages. I've always enjoyed plodding through its pyramid complex. The name

comes from a Nahua word meaning "place of twenty."
It probably refers to either twenty towns that were
part of a larger domain, or a market that occurred
every twenty days. The site is large and rarely crowded, allowing tourists to explore the complex at their
leisure. A quick glance at the site's history reinforces
how important the little village was to the conquest
of the New World.

Archaeologists currently think the pyramids
were begun about 1200 A.D., but there are hints the
site could be older. On a lower level, a clay figure
reminiscent of the Chac Mool was unearthed, indicating a possible link to the Maya. Early people lived
off agriculture, gathering, hunting and fishing in the
tributaries of the nearby Actopan River. The area
easily supported a settled population.

The pyramids of Cempoala are the only ones discovered in Mexico where people crushed seashells
and mixed the fragments with mortar in construction. These pyramids are built of roundish stones ce-
mented together. In time, Cempoala was subjugated
by the Aztecs and had to send tribute —including hu-
mans for sacrifice— to the Aztec capitol Tenochtitlan,
now Mexico City.

After Cortes landed, the Cempoalans allied themselves with the Spanish and aided in the fall of the
Aztecs. In 1520, within a walled section of the pyramid complex called Walled System IV, the Spanish
fought a major battle among themselves. Walled System IV is but a portion of the complex, but by itself
contains eighteen acres.

The result of that battle was the near total abandonment of the city by its inhabitants. In 1660, the
remaining Indians were completely removed from
the area. Cempoala still retains the stereotypical
image of the sleepy Mexican village.

96. San Juan de Ulúa. Lord let me reach that shade before I melt!

I was free to ride my motorcycle throughout the pyramid complex, stopping wherever I pleased. However, I was in for sad news this visit. I had known and become friends with a Mexican-American World War II veteran, who had retired to Cempoala, and his *compadre,* the director of the pyramid site. I always stopped every three or four years and spent several days visiting these old friends. At the entrance, I didn't see either man. When I asked for Don Huicho, they looked puzzled. I then said, *"el guía"* or "the guide." The new caretakers realized I was their old American friend. I was no longer just a tourist.

Sadly, both men had passed away since our last reunion. Learning of their deaths had a strange effect on me. I'd visited enough that we'd become true friends. Men of another nation who'd aged and died during my life. Don Huicho, a local name, spoke English as well as I did when we met but had forgotten the language over the years. They'd been in their mid-forties when I met them in 1971.

The new director took me to several homes to visit with mutual friends I knew from various fiestas and other visits. It was a sad morning with many reminiscences. Kids who had marveled at my bike in 1971 were now grown with families. My visit had been a noteworthy event in the life of the village. There had been no television and little contact with the outside world in the early '70s. My bike and white skin had broken the monotony.

Cempoala was the village I had always loved and which had provided many insights into Mexican life. This day, Los Voladores de Papantla were to perform. I had wanted to see their pre-Hispanic ritual for years. Their real home is further north at the ruins of El Tajin, but I'd always missed them when visiting in that area. I eagerly waited for three hours until the Totonac Indian troupe put on their ancient performance. For more than two hours, the Indians went through various rituals that drew little attention. A few village women appeared, herding small groups of young children. As one o' clock approached, the villagers began telling the few tourists to wait and see the unadvertised performance.

The five Indians spent thirty minutes climbing the hundred-foot-tall pole. Four of them fastened ropes to themselves and leapt from the top. The fifth Indian played his flute and drum while his partner's ropes slowly twirled through the air, lowering them to the ground. It was a performance less exciting than the rides at most county fairs and too tame to compete with an action movie. However, the fifteen to twenty tourists and thirty-plus villagers watching from the shade of a palm grove appreciated the bravery and history. They gave a hardy round of applause that echoed off the surrounding pyramid walls, saluting the Indians and their ancient tradition.

97. Palms in Cempoala.

Leaving Cempoala, I realized I hadn't eaten much seafood during this trip. I stopped at a frond-covered restaurant beside the highway and enjoyed a giant shrimp cocktail for about $3.30. Twenty years earlier, the price had been thirty-two cents. It was still a much better buy than I could have obtained in the States.

On the coastal road going north, there are a number of seaside resort hotels, especially along Costa Esmeralda, or the Emerald Coast. Architecturally, all but one of them reflect the world of 1940s movies and fit pleasantly in with the palms, banana and orange trees. The exception is a modern, multi-storied monstrosity. Thankfully, it did little business, and on this trip, appeared abandoned and physically deteriorating.

The road is great for motorcycling, curving over low mountains that melt into the seashore. Many straight stretches, mixed with slow curves, carry the rider past river villages along the way. The traffic isn't bad. You can relax and enjoy the scenery while the sun and sea air make motorcycle riding perfect.

The road changed and I started climbing into lush hills as I neared Papantla and El Tajín. The air grew sweeter and sweeter until I may as well have been driving through a vanilla spray. Papantla is the area where vanilla comes from. The crop's smell permeates the atmosphere miles before the town is reached. I enjoy Papantla, but didn't have time for the city this trip. I wanted to glance at the ruins of El Tajín, the most oriental-looking of all the indigenous Mexican civilizations. In Veracruz, I'd heard a related site had recently been discovered and I wanted to learn where it was.

I was sickened by the alterations at El Tajín. During earlier visits a few Indians lived nearby and the site was wide open. Now the pyramid complex had changed into a money-making tourist attraction. A carnival atmosphere prevailed outside the entrance. Shops selling cheap trinkets cluttered the area. For the first time, I encountered local Indians begging instead of working their farms. But once I was through the entrance, the ruins made me forget the mess outside. I toured the site until it closed and, unfortunately, couldn't find an archeologist to learn what new finds had been made.

I drove until after dark to Tuxpan (sometimes spelled Tuxpam). The last thirty miles were the worst and most poorly marked road I'd encountered this trip. I ended up arriving late at night and stayed at the Hotel Plaza Palmas. I should have looked for a cheaper one but I was in no mood to repeat the mistake I'd made in Tierra Blanca. The hotel was excellent, with a swimming pool, an interior garden and party area. There's also a night guard on duty and a tennis court, among a host of extras. The restaurant was first class, too.

98. My kind of roadside restaurant in Tabasco.

I woke after two hours of sound sleep. Perhaps it was the excitement of the trip and time running out. It was difficult to get back to sleep. I was having trouble deciding whether to head north to Brownsville, then west to El Paso to pick up my truck, or to ease northwest across Mexico's desert. I figured on three or four days extra ride staying in Mexico. I again regretted not riding the entire trip from South Carolina by motorcycle. Either route would be a bad decision. I'd have to travel 800 miles west to fetch the truck, and then cover that much distance again returning to South Carolina.

I breakfasted at the hotel with a British ship captain hired by Pemex to operate one of their tankers. It was great to converse in English. He'd arrived in Mexico only twenty-four hours earlier, and was already astounded by the differences in customs. His new bosses had immediately taken him out for a night of celebration, finally tucking him in at three in the morning. He had been up and ready, but they were already an hour and a half late when I met him. He was amazed no one was worried about getting him to his new offices on time. His conversation flip flopped from worry about the devil-may-care attitude concerning work to the hospitality and party that had followed his first meeting with company officials. I couldn't help wondering how his British background, even stricter than our American ways, would blend with Mexican culture and their attitude concerning time. Over coffee, he favorably commented on the *señoritas* he had met and the free-for-all attitude of his hosts. I thought he would be all right in the long run, for the *señoritas* had captivated the captain.

The road from Tuxpan to Tampico was terrible. There was no pavement for a forty-mile stretch. The wide dirt lane consisted of endless dips, making a wavy ride. I often rode in a self-made center lane bouncing between cars, buses and trucks that inched past each other. At one point, an independent entrepreneur was at work pretending to shovel dirt in a hole. His wife held out a basket for donations to underwrite his highway work as each vehicle eased into and out of the huge hole across the highway. This was the first stretch bad enough to make me wonder if the bike's frame could take the punishment, even at reduced speeds.

At midday, I reached the new bridge into Tampico. Even before getting on it, I again longed for the smelly, old ferry that used to carry passengers and cargo. In less than five years, the bridge already had closed lanes and was in urgent need of repair.

I rode to the cluttered city beach for a quick look before returning to El Centro for lunch. Many tourists ignore Tampico, but I enjoy the city. Mexican towns never seem to change. With a minute of reflection over coffee, I thought how true that is of Tampico. I

99. A Mexican fruit stand brimming with tropical treats in Buenos Aires, Veracruz.

stuck my hands behind my head and leaned back taking in the square and surrounding buildings. In a second, Humphrey Bogart should pass or a young Robert Blake will step up and sell me a lottery ticket. The town looks exactly like it did when *The Treasure of the Sierra Madres* was originally filmed there. So many years later, and I wonder if anything has changed.

Giving up on Bogart making an appearance, I rode the remainder of the day. South of Victoria, I watched for the mountains that would produce my 27-mile climb. The road was different. Many of the hills and curves had disappeared with the new construction. The longest distance I continually climbed was about five miles.

It was pushing night when I reached Victoria. The new road bypassed the city, so I'd have to go several miles to reach the downtown. I decided to continue instead of crossing the desert the following morning. Within thirty miles, the bright sand and scrub plants disappeared into total darkness. The night brought heavy truck traffic that resulted in four hours of tedious motorcycling.

At 1:30 a.m., July 13, I crossed the border at Brownsville, Texas. I had mixed emotions. A great adventure was ending and, despite being ready to see my family, the return to a mundane normal life wasn't overly appealing. I had covered almost 500 miles in one day. Surprisingly, the American immigration officials didn't search me.

A guard gave me bad directions, and I lost an hour getting out of Brownsville. My first ride on the freeway, even at night, was exhilarating, easy and free after Mexico. I was almost like a child playing. It's more comfortable to ride when knowing the signs and lights mean what they say. Then, I quickly recalled the other type of driving freedom in Mexico. I now had a speed limit and could get a ticket. By coincidence, I stopped at a What-A-Burger thirty miles out of Brownsville for a ham and egg sandwich and coffee. Relaxing and listening to English, I realized when I left Mexico in 1971, I'd been craving a cheeseburger for weeks. I had never heard of What-A-Burger, but it was the first place I came to in the States. Anytime I left Mexico on motorcycle, it seemed I was meant to have my first American meal in Brownsville at What-A-Burger.

The trip was a rejuvenating experience. Besides enjoying the spectacular scenery and meeting so many people, I'd answered a lot of questions about myself. I hadn't become fearful or less adventuresome with age. I could still face obstacles in a foreign culture and do fine. I continue to recommend trips to Mexico, and still find the people among the most hospitable in the world.

The rain in the mountains is a problem only if

100. Rounding any curve, be prepared to discover such a tiled roof village.

you lack a jacket and rain gear. On the early part of this trip, the Mexican coastal regions had repeatedly been hit by major storms. The clouds had covered central Mexico causing so much rain. My misery was the direct result of poor decision making on my part. For the most part, the showers are nothing but mist. Even at my coldest moments, I could have gotten off the motorcycle and been comfortable.

Despite the hour, the urge to be home was palpable. Once I left Oaxaca, there had been little stopping. I rode with new energy the remainder of the night and the next day until, fully spent, I had to rest at Sonora, Texas. I had covered 961 miles in thirty-two hours, with only stops to eat and do some quick sightseeing.

As I circled the town, an obviously expert rider exited the interstate and turned onto the road entering town. A few moments after I pulled into the little hotel, he entered too. The smooth motorcyclist turned out to be an older man.

After checking in, we introduced ourselves. He was from Galena, Texas, on his way to visit Carlsbad Caverns. We grabbed a couple of cheeseburger baskets and ate together. Ken, a small man nicknamed "Low Mate," was a 64-year-old mechanic, originally from England. He'd been riding motorcycles for 50 years. He took his vacations by making three to six day trips around the Texas area. We agreed to ride together the next morning and then, totally exhausted, I turned in.

The following morning, we rode for about 200 miles before he had to go north and I west. Ken was riding a 1986 Honda 250 in mint condition. We entered some of that strong West Texas wind, and I told him of my bike's problems. We traded bikes for ten miles and I felt like I was on a Cadillac. Ken couldn't believe how unstable my bike was and didn't know what the problem could be, only that "it will unnerve you."

It was the first time I had ridden with a partner. I found I preferred it to riding alone. It was nice having someone to share a word with when we stopped for a coke or gas. I hated riding alone again. The parting somehow emphasized the feeling my adventure was over. Despite being ready to get home, I knew I would motorcycle Mexico again. I promised myself it would be sooner than the twenty years I had let slip by since the last trip.

17. Biking Mexico in the 2000s

Strains of ZZ Top thundered above roaring motorcycle engines as I glided down the tree-shrouded lane. Dozens of bikes sprawled across a field on the right, and gleaming Harleys ushered me into the center of the gathering. A mechanical bull, a friendly crowd and Southern rock gave the sense of attending a Georgia barbeque deep in the swamp. In contrast to Monterrey and its seven million inhabitants, thirty-five miles distant, wild flowers on the low mountain plain sweetened the breeze. The only gringo at the gathering, I rode with the Templars of Saltillo.

Sexy leather-clad girls milled about as the Templars introduced me around in my first Mexican motorcycle rally. I hoped I didn't have to meet each of these Mexican good old boys immediately. An all American, "How y'all doing," wouldn't work to cover all introductions. Instead I gripped each extended hand, leaned into a light shoulder bump and the occasional hug with each greeting.

Passing from little knots of people to other groups, I learned more of the Mexican world of motorcycling. Along a brick wall in the central area, people at six stations prepared food and sold drinks. The spicy aroma of frying meat dominated the section. Every person I met asked about my travels and offered to get me a drink or a plate of food.

With their patches, tattoos, leather jackets,

101. The author enjoying a cigar at the Catemaco, Mexico, motorcycle rally.

half-gloves and a couple of guys riding with skeletal masks, this looked like the worst gang ever assembled, but the truth is far different. Mexican culture embraces costumes, and the bikers love the outlaw look but differentiate themselves from biker gangs. Riders quickly let you know they belong to clubs, not gangs. Many groups actually have a code of ethics that harken back to medieval chivalry. One code can be found at *Rage Fraternidad de Motociclistas* on Facebook. Some of the member's duties and responsibilities are translated as:

1. Be kind to women, children and animals....

2. Be nice. Back up what you say with your actions.

3. Never lie, cheat or steal.

4. Every real biker knows that his word is his value. Your word is all you have in life that is truly yours. Keep it carefully and make it a noble thing for you, because you are a true knight of the road.

5. ...help bikers, show the world that we are better than the image portrays us. Courtesy costs you nothing and gives everything. Practice what you preach.

6. You're a biker, a modern knight of the road. Protect the weak, stand tall with your head held high and proud....

Most of the bikers I met were well educated and held good jobs. The most interesting character was Luis who, despite being well tanked by evening, turned out to be a true intellectual. He caught my attention when he told another biker in Spanish, "When in doubt about making a purchase, I always say," then he switched to wonderfully accented English. "Buy American."

Luis's jacket flaunted patches representing various motorcycle rides and rallies. He'd ridden Route 66 in the States, every Mexican rider's dream. Among many notable achievements, Luis established the first National Rifle Association chapter in Mexico. Not only did Luis know how to work Mexican laws so he could possess arms, but he also knew American gun laws far better than I.

Since the turn of the century, I've mainly traveled off-road in Mexico on ATVs and written a number of articles for *Sand Sports Magazine*. One article is at: http://www.puerto-penasco.com/images/PDFS/sandsportspenasco1.pdf. I've frequently ridden motorcycles but, since 2000, never more than a hundred miles. My recent rides have been on *amigos'* bikes around different cities or when attending rallies.

As Mexico changed, the concept of motorcycling also transformed in recent years. The average North American still thinks of the Mexico I described in my first two journeys. The truth is, the country has modernized. The old Mexico exists under the surface, but today's motorcyclist also needs to know something of the modern nation before tackling the country for an adventure. When I first headed south of the border on a bike, there was virtually no automobile traffic or tractor-trailer rigs. The roads were indescribably bad. Heavily laden three-ton trucks crept along. At least nine classes of buses, belching heavy diesel smoke, ferried people. The wealthy people who owned cars drove wide open. I traveled the entire country and only saw two police cars, both in Mexico City.

On a four-wheel adventure in 2007 to a remote town two mountain ranges over from Tapalpa, Mexico, I discussed the differences in car ownership then and now. The village elder said, "We have ninety-three families in our town. In 1970, we had three pickup trucks. Today, seventy-three families own trucks."

Since 1970, virtually every Mexican city has at least tripled in population. I'd estimate auto ownership increased even more than in the remote village mentioned above. Today's rider enjoys more and better highways, but the heavier traffic makes motorcycling more dangerous.

In the 1970s, motorcycles were small and used mostly to get around in cities, but people understood someone motorcycling between towns. Such travel

102. Author with the Forasteros de Coahuila at Motofiesta in León, Guanajuato.

was seen as a need and, due to the lack of vehicles, a necessity. In 1993, I was often greeted by incredulous people, "You're motorcycling our country alone?"

As Mexico became more prosperous and the highways improved, motorcycling became more popular. Saltillo is a city approaching a million people and Eric "Rage" Vargas, an expert on motorcycling, told me the city had seventy-nine clubs in 2013. Mexico has every type club we have, but street bikes are the most popular. Like Americans, virtually everyone wants a Harley, but rides what their budget dictates. The changed attitude has given me the opportunity to ride locally with friends and attend some of the exotic rallies around Mexico.

The Mexican workweek is five and a half days. Attending distant rallies is difficult for the average rider. There are usually one or two small rallies around large cities once a month and it's hard to find a better party. Many motorcyclists leave work at midday on Saturday and camp out at these fiestas.

About every three months, most clubs will attend a rally as much as 400 miles distant. Many Mexican bikers are not wealthy. They camp out when traveling or take advantage of arrangements between clubs. Local member's homes host visiting club members. Riders usually take a Friday and Saturday off for these longer jaunts.

The average gringo will think it's pretty tough to attend a meeting 400 miles distant over a three-day weekend. However, many Mexican bikers are either fearless, absolutely insane or a combination of both. What's 400 miles when you're cruising along at over a hundred miles an hour? The uninitiated reader will think I'm joking. I'm not.

On my last trip by auto, traveling on the *autopista* south of Saltillo, I almost killed the same biker three times. I've stressed before, and do so again, knowing what's behind you when driving in Mexico is almost as important as knowing what is ahead. I was cruising at about 95 mph and started to change lanes when, thank God, I glimpsed a blur coming around me running at least 120 mph. The surprise appearance shook the heck out of me. The biker exited and got back on the highway twice more on that trip, and again passed me. Only by the grace of God did I catch a glimpse of him in the mirror each time.

* * * * *

Motofiesta, the largest motorcycle rally in Mexico, occurs in León, Guanajuato toward the end of October. A few other cities claim to host the largest event but, due to León's central location, I believe their claim. When I attended, about 15,000 bikes were parked outside the coliseum. Though most riders stayed in local hotels, plenty of tents were scattered throughout the site.

103. The Chelétaro State (Bike & Bra) Bar in Querétaro makes fellow bikers feel at home quickly.

León, the leather working center of Mexico, is a great location for rallies. Day trips to historic cities such as Guanajuato, San Miguel de Allende, Dolores Hidalgo and Querétaro are within range. I know those cities and, having enjoyed too much of the late night partying, focused on León and the rally instead of side trips.

When I attended, I drove an auto from southern Mexico and joined friends from Saltillo. Most of my time at the rally was at night. Booze and heavy metal bands dominated the dark. I was sober, but wondered how some of my companions didn't tip over hundreds of bikes as we wove our way through the crowd to visit vendors hawking everything from leather items to jewelry.

One of the best rallies I attended was in Queretaro. I had been visiting southern Mexico and my Saltillo friends texted me to meet them in Querétaro. I loaded up with fine cigars in Los Tuxtlas and drove two days to meet them at a biker bar, Chelétaro State, at 6 p.m. in the historic section of the city. We were to join up with some Querétaro motorcyclists and club members from other cities. Rage was the organizer and we were to party most of the night, then ride to nearby historic cities on Saturday. I texted Rage, saying I couldn't see how they could fit all those activities in only two days. However, I knew Mexican riders could change plans on a *peso*.

I found Chelétaro State a half hour early and entered the darkened bar. Two bartenders —Pepsiman and Tocayito— knew I was coming. Little groups of bikers filled most of the tables near the entrance. The bar split the club and a larger room with tables for smokers lay behind the bar. The sense of many sets of eyes appraising me was palpable. The couple of guys with girls quickly returned to more important pursuits, but most customers and employees assessed me as I took the last empty table. Two "top ten" waitresses worked the floor. I nodded hello to some of the watching bikers to put everyone at ease. However, if being the only gringo in the joint wasn't enough, I topped it off by ordering lemonade.

I spent my time studying the décor, customers and waitresses. An array of colorful ladies' panties hung from a frame over the counter. After my second lemonade, I asked the waitress if Pepsiman or Tocayito were around. She asked me to wait while she fetched Tocayito from the second room. We shook hands and he told me the Saltillo bikers were running late and I was to meet them at the Harley Davidson store off the *autopista* to San Luis Potosí, fifteen miles away.

I arrived a half hour before dark. A half-dozen

104. A Forasteros de Coahuila award ceremony in Querétaro with other Central Mexican motorcycle clubs.

riders milled around in front of the building. Other bikers continued to pull in and join the crowd. None of the Saltillo riders rolled in, so I finally walked over to the group and asked, "Are you waiting on the Forasteros de Coahuila?"

I was bowled over when a stocky five-foot-seven guy said, "You're Bill Kaliher, aren't you? We know about you."

We shook hands, and he introduced me all around. He said, "Two Saltillo riders had flat tires. They'll arrive soon."

Several guys said they'd seen me in Chelétaro State, but didn't know I was meeting the Forasteros. When I had a moment, I asked the fellow who had called my name how he knew me. "Rage told me about you. I follow you on Facebook."

I'd never mentioned I'd motorcycled Mexico. However, years before, an American friend traveling

105. Well dunked and drenched for my initiation into the Forasteros de Coahuila motorcycle club event in Querétaro.

with me told the proprietor of Pour la France restaurant in Saltillo I'd motorcycled the country. It turned out the owner loved motorcycles and mentioned the fact to other riders. Such information spread rapidly through the biker world in Mexico. Because I've motorcycled Mexico twice when it was considered more primitive and dangerous, I'm often granted special standing among many Mexican riders and clubs. This was a good fact to know, and perhaps explains the extra courtesies that had been extended at so many rallies.

Three hours late, the Forasteros started filtering in from Saltillo. Our original group waiting had swollen as additional riders from Querétaro and other cities joined us. Edgar "Vallarta" Cisneros and his girlfriend Lily Muñiz Ramos arrived first. I was delighted to see familiar faces. Within twenty minutes, the remainder of the Saltillo riders straggled in. Soon after, it was time to put my auto driving skills to the

106. Saluting a biker for an award.

test. At 10 p.m., the bikers headed down the crowded *autopista* wide-open. I followed as closely as possible, at about 95 mph, until exiting onto a bypass. Two miles later, I thankfully caught the tail lights of a bike exiting right, a half mile ahead. When I exited, though, nary a bike was in sight. I guessed I should turn right. Five blocks down, I spotted Don Simón and other restaurants on the right crowded with what looked like half the motorcycles in Mexico.

Rock reverberated through the night air. The Querétaro clubs had started to party hours earlier when the Saltillo riders had been expected. I met dozens of people from towns and cities throughout central Mexico. As night turned into morning, it was obvious Rage's itinerary didn't stand a chance of working out.

Somehow, I arose before midday Saturday and made my way to the countryside beyond Querétaro's suburbs. Often bridges and exits are counted differently in Mexico, but I knew the variances and found the correct rural road. I passed several typical *carne asada* restaurants —long, low buildings with ample parking and smoke rising from open fires. At the restaurant and camping site most of the Saltillo riders were relaxing and enjoying beer in a large round *palapa* thirty feet past the restaurant.

After greeting everyone, I headed eighty yards past the restaurant and ambled down a little hill to the encampment. Fifteen-foot tall, woody cactus (*Pachycereus marginatus*) with nopales mixed in left thirty-foot barren pockets, providing perfect spots for tents, outdoor cooking and partying. Eighty or so motorcycles filled the area between the cactus and the hill. While meeting many new people, I studied the setting. Recesses in the cactus offered perfect shelter from sun and wind. I envisioned cowboys and old time vaqueros camped in similar settings.

I was embarrassed many times when I failed to recall bikers I'd met over the years from other cities and rallies. Even worse, I couldn't remember all the names of people I'd met the night before. Thankfully, these good people realized it was easier to remember a lone gringo's name than for me to recall the hundred-plus I'd briefly met. The late morning gossip and visiting continued into early afternoon. It was time for a Forasteros awards ceremony, witnessed by attendees from over a dozen clubs around central Mexico.

Conversations raced in rapid Spanish, reducing my understanding to about fifty percent, but facial expressions and gestures kept me abreast of what was occurring. Beer flowed freely and the crowd roared with applause and jokes as various Forasteros received awards or patches. The jocularity increased after each presentation when the recipient ran a gauntlet while being showered by water and sprayed with fizzy soft drinks. In the midst of the fun, as the wet recipients were being razzed, two pretty girls grabbed my arms. "You need to help Rage with the next presentation," one said.

When I reached the spot, the friendly crowd circled closer and Rage said, "I think you know this is Bill. He's been with us for many years...."

I was trying to keep up with his speech when another friend stepped up and helped me into a vest. I realized I was being inducted into the Forasteros. Rage hadn't finished his remarks before the first hands grabbed me. A minute later, my new amigos had me completely soaked. I kept hollering, "Don't wet the cigar!" The cold water shocked my body in the desert air, then felt delightful. The teasing jeers increased as I studied my splattered cigar. I puffed and puffed on the damp stub. The stogie came to life with smoke despite the dunking we'd taken. The crowd roared with delight.

Late the following morning, we assembled around the main square. After many hugs and good byes, the group mounted for a ride through downtown before splitting up. The flowing river of iron delighted every child and most adults who witnessed the parade of motorcycles.

* * * * *

Although bikers will find clubs and great rallies throughout Mexico, there is one locality I want to mention for motorcyclists heading to the Yucatan. There are two main highways from Veracruz City to Villahermosa, Highway 180 or the more interior *autopista*. If you are in a rush, take the *autopista* but if you have time, Highway 180 through Los Tuxtlas might make you forget the Yucatán peninsula. Among little known beaches, archeological sites, cigar factories and a host of other attractions is the town of Catemaco. The first Catemaco motorcycle rally was held during 2013 on the *malecón* along Laguna Catemaco, a giant volcanic lake. The town closed off two blocks for biker parking. Tables and tents were set up for attendees. Los Tuxtlas would be considered remote to most first-time visitors but offers a great deal for exploring on a motorcycle. In addition to what can be accessed and enjoyed from the road, fantastic landscapes the street biker can't reach await those riding dual sport bikes.

* * * * *

Today's motorcyclists should enjoy Mexican travel no matter the choice of bike. If you're going to ride Mexico, check my Facebook page and follow some of the motorcycle clubs. You'll quickly be drawn to certain riders. Becoming friends with club members isn't necessary, but it will enhance most trips to have local bikers as friends in various regions. You know how you enjoy telling bikers visiting your town where the best biking roads are? Mexican riders are no diferent and they'll steer you —if not actually accompany you— to perfect roads you'd miss without their directions.

Section VI

Appendices

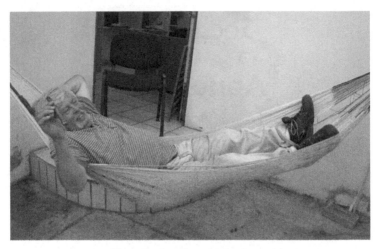
107. The author's preferred style of camping.

Mexico by Motorcyle: An Adventure Story and Guide

1. Budgeting,
Camping and Culture

I hope you enjoyed the motorcycle ride and didn't freeze in the mountains or linger in a cantina longer than I did. If you're lucky, you'll get to make such a trip and I hope your adventure and rewards are as nice as mine.

There are a thousand important aspects to Mexican travel I have not touched but, now that we're off the bike, I'd better add a bit of information.

Budgeting

Budgeting advice is difficult to provide, as prices can change rapidly in Mexico. In 1982, my wife discovered shoes in Guadalajara were selling for roughly fifteen percent of what they cost in the States. For a day or two, I thought Imelda Marcus had taken over her mind as she purchased shoes. She ensured the family would be well shod for several years —which was great, considering how fast young sons can grow. Two years later, we discovered the cost of shoes had approached American prices.

With the realization of quick price changes in mind, I'll provide some rule-of-thumb budget advice. Mexico is not the bargain store it once was but savings can be found and a vacation enjoyed at less cost than in the United States. Keep in mind, I travel on a less expensive budget than most people, as I generally want to see a lot of the country over six or more weeks rather than enjoy a luxury vacation for two weeks.

1. Border towns are different from the remainder of Mexico. There is usually a main street or area of stores that can resemble a carnival. The goal is to make as much money as possible from the one-day tourist.

2. The Maya Riviera Cancun-Tulum area is not my favorite destination and it is atypical of Mexico. I call it Miami Beach-South. A visit is comparable to a foreigner touring Disneyland and assuming it represents all of America. However, with bargain hotel and airfare available I definitely recommend the area. Nature's beauty has been perfectly sculpted for human enjoyment. This area is especially suitable for those unable to make the more arduous drive through Mexico.

3. Mexico City, Acapulco and Guadalajara are large cities and their costs are influenced by their size and by international travelers. They are more expensive than most Mexican cities but more reasonable prices can be found in the outskirts. (Mexico City, like the border towns, is not as safe as the remainder of Mexico.)

4. The next most expensive areas of Mexico are those where many Americans visit. For example, Mazatlan is a typical Mexican city except for several blocks where the cruise ships dock.

5. Auto repairs. You'll find huge savings on labor

108. Modern and traditional womanhood in Oaxaca.

when having work done on a vehicle. Parts are similar to U.S. prices and sometimes aren't in stock. If you bring a part and have it installed while in Mexico, the savings are amazing.

Generally, the larger the city and the more influenced by tourists, the higher the costs. Cities that are not tourist meccas and villages are generally less expensive. The drawback of such areas is the language barrier.

Bargaining almost anywhere is fine but don't confuse it with the type bargaining that is acceptable at border town markets. Mexicans don't ask themselves how much an item is worth, but instead, how much is this product worth to me? This is a subtle but very different approach to purchasing. The border town venders know the American mind and have a wide range of selling prices. That is not the case with the salesmen at interior markets. It is possible to offer so little for an object the vender will be insulted and refuse to discuss a sale further. So bargaining is expected, but it's not the wild freewheeling deals of the border.

When approaching a hotel clerk or a saleslady, don't hesitate to ask for a discount. Often you will get ten percent or more. People with the knowledge can get good buys, or actually make money buying gold, silver and stones south of the border. I lack that expertise, so I limit jewelry buying to reputable stores. Don't purchase cheap silver; a spread eagle and the number "92.5" on an object indicate it is sterling and is 92.5 percent pure silver.

Understandably, people think in terms of pottery, ceramics, leatherwork and native garb when shopping in Mexico. Those items are certainly abundant but, recently, the desire to produce in bulk has led to a decline in quality. However, if one searches, true quality handcrafts can still be found. If you take the time, don't be surprised to run across a papiermâché statue costing $400 USD that is a bargain. Don't limit yourself to the stereotypical assumptions concerning Mexican products. A tour of Mexican furniture stores can be eye opening. There are styles and items that are pleasing yet radically different from what is normally seen in the United States. Furnishings are often made from material not commonly employed north of the border. Carrying such items home presents a problem to a motorcyclist and often to the auto tourist. Thankfully, many of the better stores arrange shipping and shipping arrangements can also be made independently.

Check to be certain the souvenirs are not made in China. Thirty years ago, Mexico had great handcrafts but the importation of cheap Chinese handcrafts has definitely harmed Mexico's traditional handcraft production.

Camping Out

I'm reluctant to provide advice on camping in Mexico. I've been in primitive and remote areas and slept on the ground but I've never really camped in Mexico. At one time, in the open range country, one was free to drive off the road and pitch a tent. Today, you'd probably be safe staying just off the main highways but why risk being in sight should drug smugglers pass? In emergencies, I recommend driving a few miles down one of the side roads running to a distant village off the main highways. Find a secluded spot where you can pull off and pitch a tent behind the cactus, mesquite and scrub. The main problem, even away from the main highway would probably be passing herders or villagers who decide to sit down and wait for morning to see what you do. I have pulled off the highway to sleep more than once in what I felt was a remote and hidden spot, only to unwittingly attract an audience. A complete newcomer to Mexico should only camp as I'm suggesting if there is no other option. There is more concern about random crime in Mexico than was the case on my long journeys. Many RVers park at Pemex stations and tip the attendants a few dollars to watch out for them. However, if it's not one night roadside camping and you're entering remote territory, then you need far more than this guide.

The equipment you choose will depend on the geographical area. Deserts, barren mountains, forested mountains and tropical forests all demand some differences in planning and camping preparation. There is a world of difference between the Great Chihuahuan Desert, the Yucatan jungle and the Sierra Madre Occidental. Many areas are remote enough that it is not exceedingly difficult to encounter natives who have never seen a white, yellow or black person.

In the mountainous areas, one has to be prepared to camp in any conditions. It is possible to sleep in a desert terrain one night and hike or bike to forests where it can snow. Additionally, hunters tell me Mexico has more big cats than we have in the States. Fortunately, I've never encountered large cats but there have been many times eagles soaring fifteen feet above me while motorcycling made me nervous. I'm certain it would be more unsettling while on foot. Additionally, one must be aware of snakes and scorpions.

If you are planning to camp, especially in remote areas, make sure your tent is one piece. You don't want scorpions entering during the night. Never sleep in an arroyo or a dry riverbed. For more information on Mexican camping, there are several sources on the internet. Professor Jeffery R. Bacon offers some excellent advice at: http://www.mexconnect.com/mex_/travel/jrbaccon/jrbcamping.html

Mexican Culture and Customs

Let's say you have to move tomorrow. You need some help moving your furniture and ask your Mexican friend to help. He has tickets to a bullfight he's not going to miss for anything, but he says he'll help you. You get mad at your buddy for not showing up. You fume and he enjoys the bullfight, never giving your predicament a second thought. We have one of the clashes between Mexican and American thinking that can be exasperating. But there is an explanation.

Some years ago, I was with some Mexican friends. I innocently answered a question, "No. I'm sorry, I can't pick you up tomorrow."

Later, I stopped at a restaurant with one of the

group, a friend fluent in English and with a great understanding of American customs. We ordered and he said, "I wish I could do that."

I hadn't done anything and looked about to see if I'd accomplished something I was completely unaware of. Unfortunately, the women were not standing in a stupor at my magnificent masculinity nor had the men gathered to recognize me as the true heir to the throne. Confused I said, "Do what?"

He set his glass down and said, "Say no."

"Do what?" I asked, more puzzled than ever.

"You told Ricardo 'No, you couldn't pick him up.'"

"Well I couldn't. I'd already promised to visit your family in the morning."

"We cannot say no. It would be much easier if we could."

"What do you mean you can't say no?"

"It would hurt the person's feelings."

I spent a good deal of time getting a full explanation. My friend was simply amazed we Americans could say "no" so easily. He admired us for the ability and flatly stated it would be a useful thing in Mexico. At the same time, in his culture it would be an insult. It was much better to tell a white lie, "Yes, I'll help you move tomorrow," rather than hurt the person's feelings by stating you had another obligation or something more important to do.

I've found many minor cultural conflicts result from a misinterpretation of the other person's customs. I still get annoyed when I'm stood up by a Mexican friend, but now at least I realize he was sparing my feelings when he said he'd meet me. I've alluded to other different aspects of Mexican thinking —the Malinche complex, time and purchasing. Even now, after many years visiting Mexico, I'm still not aware of all the things I do that Mexicans interpret differently than I intended. However, I've learned to go a bit slower, have more patience and realize something I might not like isn't necessarily an insult. Luckily, most Mexicans fully realize our customs are different and, although they may not approve of some of our ways, most make allowances for our strange actions like saying "no" or expecting someone be on time.

In Summary

There are many reasons to visit Mexico — the scenery, historical sites, handcrafts, the food, shopping, ancient European or colonial cities, the Indian ruins and pyramids— but the people are the best of all. If you've been thinking of taking that trip south of the border, I encourage you. Whether by motorcycle or auto, it can be a sometimes grueling test, but you'll discover unimagined delights. When you return, you will have had a true adventure and a feeling of having accomplished a sometimes difficult but wonderful task.

* * * * *

You may reach the author at: wkalihcr@gmail.com, friend him on Facebook to view additional photographs or follow him on twitter: https://twitter.com/#!/WilliamKaliher, or find more information at billsmexicantours.com

2. Trip Log

1993 (Approximate Dates)

June 19   Left South Carolina for Santa Fe, New Mexico

June 24   Truck stored and left El Paso for bank and border crossing; departed Juárez about noon, Mexican time, Highway 45; dunes on edge of Great Chihuahuan desert about 1 pm; break at small town at about 85 miles; first toll road at about 100 miles.

Reached Chihuahua at nightfall.

June 25   Left Chihuahua at 8:30 am; lunch at Cárdenas; at Delicias took free road to Ciudad Camargo Jiménez, debated detouring; made 276 miles stopping at Bermejillo to spend night.

June 26   Left Bermejillo at 7 am; only made 85 miles by 10 am due to high winds; made four more stops for warmth during morning; drenched in rolling hill country; stopped for day 75 miles before Fresnillo; spent afternoon visiting small towns of Juan Aldama and Miguel Auza.

June 27   Left for Fresnillo early; enjoyed a long lunch in town of Felix U. Unger; stopped Fresnillo; reached Zacatecas after dark.

June 28	Up at 7:30 am.
June 29	Up at 8 am.; visited La Quemada; drove to Aguascalientes.
June 30	Visited Cathedral and churches; left at noon; did 100 miles by 4:30 p.m.; spent afternoon and night at Tepatitlán.
July 1	Arrived in Guadalajara.
July 4	Visited Tonalá market; spent night in Tepatitlán.
July 5	Headed for Morelia; took secondary and farm roads through Arandas and Irapuato to Salamanca.
July 6	Left Salamanca at 7 am; made three stops in forty miles to warm up —stopped at Laguna de Yuriria and Laguna de Cuitzeo to watch fishermen and get warm; visited aquaduct in Morelia and got bike serviced; reached Atlacomulco to spend night.
July 7	Cold miserable start, stopped four times for warmth in reaching Toluca; took back roads through national park during horrible storm to reach Cuernavaca and then onto Cuatla.
July 8	Left at 10 am and traveled until thirty minutes before dark in reaching Oaxaca.
July 9	Visited Monte Albán and found old road to city.
July 10	Oaxaca to Tierra Blanca via Tuxtepec, rented room in brothel.
July 11	Visited Boca del Río and Veracruz.

July 12	Rode to Veracruz; visited San Juan de Ulua; steamy hot weather; ate supper at a Western style restaurant with a Confederate flag out front.
July 13	Headed north on highway 180; visited Cempoala, where first Christian cross was raised on mainland of N. America; discovered old friends had died; left for Papantla and El Tajín and spent night in Tuxpan.
July 14	Breakfasted with British sea captain and went to Tampico; decided to leave Tampico in early afternoon and head north.
July 15	Crossed border at Brownsville, Texas.

1971 (Approximate Dates)

June 1	Crossed border at Brownsville/Matamoros.
June 3	Spent night in Torreón.
June 4-5	Traveled to Mexico City; camped out.
June 24	Left Mexico City 5 pm; crossed mountainous road to Veracruz; stopped for hours during horrific landslide.
June 25	Traveled south of Cempoala.
June 29	Veracruz.
June 30	Headed south through Lerdo de Tejada, La Venta, Comalcalco to Villahermosa.
July 1	Frontera, Campeche, had hottest pepper ever tasted; spent night at Ciudad del Carmen.

July 2	Traveled unpopulated beach for hours, coconut orchards, native huts and two Maya boys spear fishing; reached Merida.
July 3-4	Mérida.
July 5	Progresso and Extoul.
July 7-11	Stayed at Extoul, visited Dzibilchaltun, Uxmal.
July 12	Traveled to Izamal; slept at station.
July 13	Chichén Itzá and Valladolid, traveled through the night and slept on sand at Carribean sea.
July 14	Left; saw stranded European tourists; reached Tulum and continued on to sleep among unexplored ruins.
July 15	Reached Chetumal, free city, spent night.
July 16	Left perhaps 2 pm, long ride; stopped Xpuil, bike trouble in jungle; reached station and slept.
July 17	Interesting breakfast with Maya highway workers, rode to Palenque and slept at ruins.
July 18	Traveled Highway 199 toward San Cristóbal de la Casas to Cascadas de Agua Azul, then long hard ride to Villahermosa.
July 19	Stopped at Minatitlán for bike repair on return to Veracruz.
July 20-21	Veracruz
July 22-27	Cempoala

July 28-31 Costa Esmeralda

August 1-4 Papantla and El Tajín

August 5 Tampico

August 6 Traveled to Victoria

109. The author tries out a bike before the trip.

3. Basic Bike Information

If your planned trip will carry you beyond the main roads and cities, the following assortment of equipment is critical for roadside repairs. Supplement this list with your own choices and suggestions made by your dealer. They do know what breaks on every bike they sell.

Unless you are a good mechanic, don't travel to Mexico without a basic, easy-to-understand repair manual. If you don't have one, ask your dealer for the company's detailed upkeep and minor repair manual or the shop manual.

At a minimum, an adjustable wrench should supplement your bike's tool pouch. I suggest taking tools to make your own repairs if a breakdown occurs, particularly any specialty tools. Wrenches, allen wrenches and sockets take very little storage room. The tool kit delivered with most bikes is of limited use when making repairs. You may also need the following:

1. A small flashlight that stores easily

2. A multi-use tool such as a Gerber tool or a Leatherman

3. A small tire pump

4. Two large box end wrenches needed for chain

adjustment

5. Gasket compound such as Prema-Tex

6. Extra fuses

7. A small can of oil

8. Chain wax

9. A small can of penetrating oil

10. A few chain links or an extra chain

11. Extra spark plugs

12. A can of Fix-A-Flat (I've had a flat from a thorn.)

13. Chain or cable and a good lock

4. Preparation List and Extra Items

This is a basic check list for motorcycling Mexico on an extended trip. Your list will vary. A three to seven day short jaunt into Mexico would not require as much preparation and planning.

Double check entry requirements one week before departure

Advise your bank that you will be using your ATM card and credit cards in Mexico

Make certain your credit card is in your wallet

Make a small packet to contain your identification, entry and exit paperwork and traveler's checks

Pack:

A few ziplock bags to store and protect other items

A notebook to list details and for labeling photographs

Shield for helmet

Bike tools

Laptop

Bill Kahlier's book

Your bike's shop manual

Pocketknife

Flashlight

Digital camera & cable

Batteries

Hair brush

One pair good pants, jeans, socks, underwear, tee-shirts, good shirts, sneakers, boots
Warm coat

Rainsuit

Spanish dictionary/software

Bug spray and mosquito netting, if entering primitive areas

One towel and face cloth

Lighters

Fuses for bike

Maps

Touring guide

Plastic poncho that can serve as a ground cloth

Blanket

First aid kit

Prescription medicines

Malerial medicines if traveling to an at risk area

I wouldn't carry items such as, Chapstick, Advil, vitamins, and antacids. They can be purchased as needed in Mexico.

Any list depends on each traveler and what he or she wants to accomplish. This book is aimed at the motorcyclist who doesn't have the option of extra space. I urge riders to ensure these basics are packed before adding other equipment.

However, when preparing, common sense and background knowledge can alter any list. I normally purchase a Mexican blanket while traveling, which I use for seat padding and sleeping if needed. If I wasn't going to purchase a native blanket I'd pack a blanket and wrap it in my poncho.

The most important item listed is, of course, Bill Kaliher's book. The rider can consult it and say, "Hey Kaliher doesn't know as much about Mexico as he thinks. He didn't tell me the girls were this beautiful." At other times, when he's lost in a city, he can cuss me and say, "Darn, Kaliher didn't tell me how to say "Where is the main highway." He'll, of course, be correct. No book can provide information for every situation.

This book should give you a good feel for the country, but definitely supplement what is imparted here with other information concerning Mexico.

110. Singing songs from the early 20th century with an herbalist in Los Organos, Veracruz. Pack versatile clothing in case you find yourself performing.

5. Clothing

With a motorcycle, storage space is everything. On a long tour, the rider can face temperatures ranging from burning desert to cold mountainous driving. I now realize I did a better job of clothing preparation on my first Mexican motorcycle trip than I did on my second tour. I was overconfident concerning clothes when preparing for the second journey.

The rider may want to play with these suggestions to gain room. Rain gear is a must and yet some rain suits require too much room. An army poncho that can also serve as a ground cloth or made into a small tent is an excellent replacement for a standard rain suit. The problem with the poncho is it has to be tied around the waist or tucked under the rider's legs when traveling and does not protect the lower legs. Still, the poncho can serve several other purposes when it's not raining and only rain gear for the legs is needed. On my second trip, I took a plastic poncho but it wasn't as good as the variety the army uses. The wind quickly ripped it to tatters.

I've provided a minimum list of clothing for a month-long trip if the rider plans to keep moving. Adjust it for your trip and needs.

If your journey is strictly along the coasts, you won't need the warmer clothes. If you're planning to stay in one place for a week at a time, cleaning clothes will be easier and less are required. Once you're packed, cram the extra space with clothes you can throw away. Wear them first and then lighten your load by leaving them.

Additionally, think about what Mexican wear you plan to purchase that can be used on the trip. If you're certain you're going to obtain some Mexican-style shirts, ponchos or pants, then carry fewer of these to start.

The following list is suggested for trips lasting two to six weeks and applies to men as well as women:

A warm leather jacket

A sweater if there's space

A rainsuit or good poncho

Two pairs of jeans besides the pair you're wearing

Six short-sleeve or tee shirts

Six changes of socks and underclothes

A pair of shorts that can double as a bathing suit

One pair of pants for fine dining or a good skirt if you have room

Two-long sleeve shirts. One shirt or blouse to go with the dress slacks or skirt. The second long-sleeve shirt will protect your arms from sunburn while riding.

A pair of tennis shoes to supplement your boots

Add socks and underclothes if you have room

Index

to cities, towns and geographical areas by page

Made in the USA
Las Vegas, NV
05 January 2021